RELENTLESS
STATE OF MIND

THE POWER OF MENTAL CONDITIONING

RELENTLESS

STATE OF MIND

KEVIN ARMENTROUT

LAS VEGAS

ARMENTROUT
Las Vegas, Nevada

For information please contact support@kevinarmentrout.com
or visit www.kevinarmentrout.com

First Hardcover Edition December 2017

This book is written as a source of information only. The information contained in this book should by no means be considered a substitute for the advice of a qualified medical professional, who should always be consulted before beginning any diet, exercise, health, or wellness program.

All efforts have been made to ensure the accuracy of the information contained in this book as of the date published. The author disclaims liability for any adverse effects that may occur as a result of applying the methods suggested in this book.

Scripture quotations are from the ESV® Bible
(The Holy Bible, English Standard Version®), copyright © 2001
by Crossway, a publishing ministry of Good News Publishers.
Used by permission. All rights reserved.

Photo Credit: Joan Rodriguez Garcia

PRINTED IN THE UNITED STATES OF AMERICA

17   18   19   20   21   5   4   3   2   1

Library of Congress Cataloging-in-Publication Data: 2017917527

ISBN – 978-1-5323-6042-8
ISBN – 978-1-5323-6043-5 (eBook)

FOR THE WARRIOR SEEKING PURPOSE WITHOUT WAR

CONTENTS

CONTENTS

Finally, brothers, whatever is true, whatever is honorable, whatever is pure, whatever is lovely, whatever is commendable, if there is any excellence, if there is anything worthy of praise, think about these things.

✝ Philippians 4:8

ACKNOWLEDGEMENTS

I thank everyone who has helped mold and shape my mind along the way. These are some of the most influential.

My Mother
The most selfless person I have ever met. I used to think you didn't understand how much you gave of yourself, and how it affected your life. I now know I just didn't understand life.

Lawrence J. Rinetti
You were the first one to introduce me to the importance of mindset, not just in dynamic entries but in life. You taught me to stand as a leader and look adversity in the eye.

Tony Robbins
You helped me understand where I was and where I wanted to be. You gave me the opportunity to see my greatest aspirations first hand. You've helped me rewrite my story.

My Wife
You have patiently stood by my side at the corner of every crossroad. You continue to be my biggest supporter and my guiding light. Without you I'm not sure where I would be, but I know it couldn't nearly be as good as this.

CHAPTER 1
INSIDE THE HUMAN MIND

The whole of science is nothing more than a refinement of everyday thinking.

— Albert Einstein

Wouldn't it be great to be able to master your surroundings, control your environment, and shape the outcomes of your life? You're damn right it would be. Even better, is it can be. You can shape who you are, build who you want to be, and embody the values of your very soul. This all begins in the center of our minds, in our every thought, and in every behavior, both conscious and not. These thoughts, these dispositions, shape the very nature of our being. From the innermost workings of our brains, comes the very nature of who we are as people. So much of you, and what is happening around you, is derived from your every thought.

It is more commonly understood that our thoughts can alter our mood or change our outlook; but what if you realized that they were far more controlling than that? What if you came to understand that your thoughts and mental process controlled your surroundings as well? People, situations, opportunities, all are affected by your thinking. Just like James Allen's *As a Man Thinketh*, I will show you how your thoughts have far more influence on your outcome than you may think, and bring you a whole new meaning to the term mind control. You will come to understand the power of thought, the processes involved in disrupting your current patterns, and the path to building new ones.

Before we go any further, I want you to understand that this book, and this process, is not about positive thinking. I repeat this is not about positive thinking. This is not the power of, or better yet, the lack of power in positive thinking. This is the power of knowledge, followed by action. You cannot merely sit around thinking about an object or an idea, and magically bring that thought to fruition. Saying over and over, "I don't receive bills, I don't receive bills, I don't receive bills…" is only going to disappoint you when you go and check the mail later. Dreaming about success will only make you successful when your head hits the pillow at night, and praying for money is so religiously foul and misguided that you need to remove that thought from ever crossing your mind. This book is about real scientific information coupled with real and immediate behavior. That is where the power in this process lies. Learning and understanding how your mind works, and then putting that knowledge into decisive action. I have been able to listen to Tony Robbins, an expert in this area, say many times, "Knowing is not enough! You must take action."

Over the last year, I've had the privilege of working with Tony as a guest speaker, and it's had a significant impact on my life. During one of his seminars, I had a profound moment when I realized that the majority of my life had been spent learning, utilizing, and teaching on one central aspect of the human psyche. For nearly 20 years, instructing on mindset, and training in mental conditioning has been at the forefront of my career. Dissecting, understanding, and implementing tactics and procedures, in attempts to create the perfect mindset, has been my sole focus. More than 15 of those years I had spent in and with the United States Marine Corps. I spent the majority of my military career studying and training, to achieve the perfect mindset during combat operations. The goal was to obtain a peak mental state that did not falter under adversity, that was conditioned to chaos and primed for battle, that did not act on emotion, but used rationale and intelligence above all else. I can't give you an exact statistic to my success, but I can assure you that it was well tested in combat.

I spent many years, after leaving the service, instructing Marines deploying to Iraq and Afghanistan. I found within each scenario and training environment, that I always focused more on the conditioning of the mind, and less on the individual tactics. It was evident that no matter the amount of training a Marine had gone through, a lack of mental conditioning made it almost irrelevant. I did my best to teach in a way that would provide knowledge, explain the action that needed to be taken, but most importantly, set the stage for the mindset that needed to be present for the greatest success. That was my main outlook and ongoing role as a leader of Marines. The focus was, **not how do I become successful as a leader, but how do I create success in those I lead.**

During that same time, I began to lead people to succeed with their health and fitness goals as well. I would provide knowledge and information, create strategies and plans, and for some, be right there face to face pushing them to their goals. It wasn't long before I realized the key to the majority of my clients' health and fitness goals wasn't the detailed plan I had provided them. It was the mindset they had going into it. Their thought process had more of a determining factor than any diet or exercise program. Here I was in a completely different field and operating under identical principles. No matter the amount of knowledge, information, and programing that was available to my clients, a lack of mental conditioning made it all seem irrelevant. So, I began to coach less on the effect of their nutrition and more on the impact of their beliefs that were associated with it. I started to focus less on their metabolic conditioning and more on their mental conditioning. This is where the real success began to happen. The power didn't lie in their exercise programing but in their thought process. Mindset was critical; mindset was everything!

○   ○   ○

The real power in your thoughts comes from the immense amount of power you have in your brain, that perfectly engineered mainframe you carry around in your head. This biological supercomputer that contains billions upon billions of neurons controlling every aspect of human anatomy is right there at your disposal, anytime you want to use it. The problem with most of us is that we tend not to. Not that we don't use it at all, but that we don't use it correctly. We tend to limit our minds growth, fall victim to certain beliefs, we're hesitant with fear and fail to align our thoughts with our purpose. We never see our mind's full potential, thus never truly seeing our own.

See, the human mind is one of God's most beautiful creations. It has a fantastic ability to learn, adapt, and to survive! That is the big one, survival. The mind has so many different aspects of survival and adaptability built into it, that it truly is astonishing. Just like Artificial Intelligence (AI) of today's supercomputers, which are continuously seeking and learning information to adjust and function at higher levels, so is your brain. The only difference, between AI and you, is that you're not artificial! You're real, and your mind is always seeking and learning new information whether you like it or not. So, the real issue that comes to hand, is what information are you giving your brain to learn from?

I'll take a page of James Allen and illustrate your mind to you as a gardener in his garden. You are the gardener, and the garden is your mind. No matter what, the garden is going to grow, just as your mind will grow. If the gardener plants bad seeds, then his garden will bear bad fruit. So is the same with good seed, and good fruit. What you plant in your mind will grow, and you have the ability to plant whatever seeds you'd like. If the gardener tends to his garden daily, watering and

6

nurturing it, then it will surely flourish. However, if he neglects it, the weeds will certainly take over his garden. This is no different than you, feeding your mind what it needs every day to flourish. If you let your mind go, and allow the mindless nonsense of our generation to consume it, the weeds will surely grow!

"It was the best of times, it was the worst of times, it was the age of wisdom, it was the age of foolishness..."

— Charles Dickens, *A Tale of Two Cities* (1859)

I couldn't agree more with Mr. Dickens's famous opening sentence. Now, we aren't amidst a French Revolution, but trust me when I tell you, we are in a revolution. You are living amongst the technological revolution that will be referred to as such in the history books to come. Many men and women didn't realize the profound nature of the era they were living in during the industrial revolution. The same can be said today of our society and the technological world. From 2000-2050, we will see technology go from the birth of the internet to the advancement of not just smartphones, smart cars, and smart homes, but entire smart cities. Technology will bring automation to everything we own, information at our fingertips faster than you can ask for it, and it all will be seamlessly integrated as one.

This can be the best of times, and an age of wisdom as we move forward; this can be a very dark time in our society and an era of diminishing intelligence and foolish behavior. I assume it will be an unbalanced mixture of both. As things become more and more automated as simple and mundane tasks are made easier and more efficient, we have the opportunity as a society to become more enlightened individuals or seemingly mindless as a whole. Advancements in technology give us the ability to seek and learn new information on a whim in a moment's notice. Technology also brings information into our lives, wanted or not, at an alarming rate. I'm talking about good seeds, bad seeds, and everything in between. This will all boil down to how well you manage the weeds.

Your brain, that supercomputer we talked about before, works a lot like the real computers of today, sending and receiving information, communicating at lightning speeds, calculating and processing every second of the day. We walk around with devices in our hands that provide constant and endless information. We have television services that literally offer thousands of channels of entertainment. We have games of every kind, on every platform. Social media, streaming video, news feeds, games and apps, are all right there in the palm of our hands. Everything you view, read, play, and interact with, your brain is taking in, interpreting, storing, and learning from. Everything! I am not some old and outdated hater of technology; I'm quite the opposite. I want you to embrace the advancements in technology and the information available to you, while warning you of the seemingly harmless, yet mind-numbing content that continually streams in our direction.

Your mind, your garden, it wants to be watered. It needs it every day. If you don't supply it, it will find it. In today's society, unless you attempt to move to a remote island and live like Tom Hanks in *Cast Away*, you cannot hide from information. So, you must choose the information you take in. You must filter the water you give to your garden. Understanding that your mind is always taking in information, and how to increase your mind's ability to retain specific information, is key. I'm going to give you a blueprint of your brain, look at fixed and growth mindsets, and provide you tools like the rule of three and priming, to maximize your mind's full potential.

O   O   O

The "Rule of Three" is a writing principle and the understanding of the brain's ideal communication and its adaptive response to information. This concept has a long-standing history in everything from literature and film, to military and law. Depending on the person you're discussing this subject with, will significantly determine their outlook on it. The interesting part, is that they are all correct. Through countless different studies, the brain has shown to have an increased memory association with groups of three. In turn making things that are visually paired in groups of three more appealing. The simplest way to put this is your brain views, memorizes, and recalls things in groups of three. When you are presented something, your brain likes it in three's. When given information, your brain will store it in three's. When all hell breaks loose, your brain will recall any emergency procedures in three's. Go ahead and think about things that you've memorized without effort over the years.

- 911
- Stop, Drop, & Roll
- Lights, Camera, Action
- Shout, Show, Shove
- Ready, Set, Go
- Stop, Look, Listen
- Bigger, Faster, Stronger
- Ready, Aim, Fire
- Mind, Body, Soul
- Blood, Sweat, & Tears

I could go on and on, but I think you get the point. Think about some of the most profound statements in history, like Thomas Jefferson's, "life, liberty, and the pursuit of happiness," or Abraham Lincoln's "of the people, by the people, for the people." Your brain communicates in patterns. In fact, it is always trying to find and decipher patterns, and the pattern it communicates the best with... You guessed it, three!

What you take into your mind, can and will affect those patterns. Thought patterns can and will affect your mood, your emotions, your perception, and disposition. All those things, can and will affect your daily interactions, the people around you, your surroundings, opportunities, and even your outcome. You may ask, how can a single thought change your surroundings and control your outcome? Simple really. You are a creature of habit. You are a being of your thoughts. Your thoughts are widely influenced by the information your brain takes in on a daily basis.

Have you ever met someone that no matter the instance, they just seem to make the best of every situation? They constantly have a smile on their face, so pleasant to be around, and always seem to be doing well. Have you ever met someone that is the exact opposite, in that no matter the circumstances, they are just miserable to be around? They seem hard to please, incessantly complaining about their situation or surroundings, and it just seems like they can never catch a break. Do you think these two people have a completely different biological makeup? Do you think one is more privileged than the other? No, they are simply beings of their thoughts. They are products of their minds, more specifically, their mindset.

In theory, we can categorize these into two basic approaches, **a fixed mindset versus a growth mindset.** Mindset is merely a belief system that dictates how we respond to specific criteria. Our overall mindset will usually carry similar characteristics throughout. Meaning that our thinking tends to be similar in different areas of life, based on our belief systems. In a fixed mindset, a person is more prone to limiting behaviors. Hence the term fixed. This type of mentality is convinced of certain innate characteristics about themselves, their abilities, and the world around them. They tend to believe that their intelligence and talents are fixed traits. When these characteristics are contested, that person tends to become very defensive. Their beliefs have been challenged, and it's a very natural but negative response. Worse yet, it can cause that person to pick up certain limiting behaviors, solely for the purpose of confirming those beliefs within themselves.

A fixed mindset seeks information to confirm their beliefs and behaviors, and allows conflicting material to anger and upset them. These thoughts of negativity can adversely affect their disposition. That sort of character shows in a person, affecting their surroundings, limiting their opportunities, and distancing those around them. These limiting effects then drive more adverse thoughts, completing the pattern, and building a habit. All starting from a single thought.

On the other hand, the person of a growth mindset, that seems to have an abundance of joy, and an optimistic outlook also does so through thought. A growth mindset has a disposition of our individual characteristics not being fixed, but rather the ability to improve. Contrasting or conflicting information can be seen with optimism and a potential for progress. This type of personality is inviting to those around them. Surroundings are still affected, but now opportunities present themselves. People want to do business with a person with that type of energy and influence. Relationships seem to flourish, and it's hard not to remain optimistic, and feel in control of your outcome. Another pattern, another habit, and another thought.

The concept of these two different mindsets was developed by Carol S. Dweck, professor of psychology at Stanford University. She has spent years studying the effects, learning capacities and successes associated with each type of mindset. The main point to take away from her research is the growth mindset's ability to learn. A firm understanding that talents and intelligence are things that can improve over time is the key here. This mindset allows us to view perceived failures and blunders with a different outlook, and that of an optimistic opportunity for learning and improvement. This means that each setback, failed attempt, or answer of "no" is only viewed as one more thing learned, one less strategy to try, and one less person to ask. A growth mindset can pave the way for success because it operates under the premise – *Not yet*. A growth mindset is relentless.

11

As I said before, this isn't about sitting around and telling yourself that you're a happy person. This isn't positive thinking; it's not even the law of attraction. Those ideas are appealing and sound simple enough. Think this, and I'll receive that. Almost a sort of karma, do good things and good things happen in return. The problem is, our lives just aren't that simple. We are more complex; our minds and thoughts are more complex. So, how do we attempt to control every thought that comes into our minds? Well, we don't. What we do try to do, is understand ourselves at the highest levels. That's precisely what this book is about. This is understanding, in vivid detail, the process of knowing your outcome. Honest assessments of who, and where you want to be. Removing things and surroundings from your life that limit you. Manipulating your environment in order to influence the subconscious. Breeding habitual practices that will initiate positive action. Filtering information and feeding your mind. Creating a balance within yourself, resulting in the purest form of thought.

Throughout this book, I am going to introduce you to an entire process of creating the appropriate mindset to succeed in any environment. I will reference health and fitness often, but this process will work and can be applied to any aspect of life. I focus on your health and fitness because it is essential to daily living, relatable to everyone, and provides the biggest residual impact to other areas of life. I will lay out the method of thought patterns, the rule of three, and the impact of priming throughout the entire process. You'll learn about creating habitual practices and understanding the power of grace. I will discuss with you the keys to breakthrough, taught to me by Tony Robbins, which changed the way I looked at my entire approach to coaching and the inspiration for this book. This book will guide you through mind, body, and soul, understanding thought, its effect on your health, and its impact on your faith. I will walk you through all three stages of the program, each having three distinct steps in each stage. You will end with a powerful understanding of yourself, a wealth of knowledge, and a decisive action plan. You will recognize that your mindset is everything. You will leave with a *Relentless State of Mind*.

CHAPTER 2

UNDERSTANDING YOU

Knowing others is wisdom, knowing yourself is enlightenment.

— Lao Tzu

Taking a step back and asking yourself where and who you really are, is never an easy task. We have a difficult time being judgmental and critical of ourselves. We tend to exaggerate certain perceptions of ourselves, and are bias to our particular behaviors. None of this is uncommon and quite honestly, perfectly ok. In this chapter, I want you to understand where you are at in your life, but more importantly where you want to go. Where you want to be is far more significant than where you are at right now. This is why I'm not going to really ask you to evaluate who you are and where you are. What I am going to ask you to do is to take a good hard look at where you want to go, and who you want to be when you get there. That within itself will give you a good understanding of where you're at right now. Sitting around and picking out your flaws and writing down everything you hate about yourself isn't the best therapy. Trust me; I've done it. It honestly doesn't matter where you're at right now, just where you want to go. The starting point is irrelevant to the destination.

Just as with every fitness client I've ever had, their starting weight or body type never really mattered. What did matter was the goal ahead and the journey we were about to take to get there. Instead of picking out everything they were doing wrong, we focused on everything that needed to happen to make things right. That's the same exact approach to what we are going to do with you here. You're going to take an honest assessment, not of what's wrong with who or where you are in life, but what you would ultimately like to see happen in your life.

O   O   O

We're talking about goals, big goals, and the ones you want to achieve personally. Google defines the term goal as: "the object of a person's ambition or effort." Ugh, an object. We all too often associate a goal with an object, but it should be so much more than that. Our goals need to be deeper in meaning to carry any real weight. Merriam-Webster starts to get us a little closer with "the end towards which effort is directed." The end, a pinnacle of our efforts. Doesn't that lead us to believe that at some point our efforts will stop? We would need a new goal to put our efforts towards again, and again, and again. What if the goal was more significant than that? What about a goal that effort could always be applied to, not because it was unattainable, but rather that is was deeper than just an object or an end?

To give you some perspective of where we're going, let me give you an example. Every time a fitness client gave me a goal like "I want to lose weight," I would tell them, "Great, we can do that today!" I would explain to them, that in one session they will have probably lost a few ounces, maybe even a pound (in water weight), and that they would have officially lost weight. Goal accomplished, you can make that check payable to Kevin Armentrout. Usually, the client would understand where I was going and that their goals needed to be specific, have real meaning, and something that will hold them accountable. That would then turn into something like, "I want to lose 50 pounds," which I would immediately respond with "No you don't."

I would get some pretty odd glares in return, mostly with a look of "who are you to tell me what my goals are?" I would tell them the number is just a number. I wanted to know what they really wanted. That was the *what*; I wanted to know the *why*. No one wakes up and says I want to lose weight. What does happen is someone gets tired of certain aspects in their life. Someone has something significant they would like to achieve in their life. They have a change that needs to happen in their life. That weight, that 50 pounds is what they believe to be the one thing that will bring it to fruition for them. See, the goal is to never lose weight, or gain weight (muscle), or tone up, or any other arbitrary statement. The goals I always ended up hearing were to be able to play sports with their children, to look attractive for a spouse, to improve a serious health condition, be a parent a child could be proud of, and so many others. These were the real goals. These are what my clients and I set forth to accomplish, the 50 pounds just so happened to be lost along the way.

This tendency to have, what I call "surface goals," is often the same in other areas of life as well. We limit our goals and ambitions in terms of generalities. Surface goals are simple things like get rich, buy a dream home, get married, or start a business. We end up revealing what is merely on the surface, describing our goals in general monetary values or possessions, reducing them to single moments in time, and ultimately diminishing their true purpose. It's like saying lose weight. Fine, go to the bathroom, come back and you've lost weight. Great job, goal accomplished, now go away. **Goals without meaning, are goals without means.**

Just like with weight-loss, you can merely say, "I want to make more money." Fine, here's a dollar, now go away. You have to take those same goals and dig beneath the surface, find the deeper meaning, and define the real intent within them. To get rich or to attain a level of financial freedom that allows you to have peace of mind and certainty in your future? To buy a dream home or to invest in a place to build family memories that will last a lifetime? To get married or to connect with another human being on unimaginable levels of thought and emotion? To start a business or to build on a passion that drives you to make a difference each and every day? In each of these scenarios, the latter gives meaning and depth to an otherwise general and unconvincing statement.

I want you to understand that this is an important step when trying to understand what it is that you really want. So many of us have these goals that are just objects, mere possessions. When all actuality they are just achievements. We tend to place this immense amount of value in an object. We do so because we connect with the feeling we think that thing will bring us. We begin to believe that if we could only achieve this one thing, it would fix everything else. That if we could just make more money, buy a bigger home, or have a better body, we would be happier, or more productive, or a better person. What we fail to understand is the difference between feeling happy and a state of happiness. Don't get it confused, they are different. When we chase that feeling, we tend to make what I call "feel goals." This is a goal that is attached to the perceived feeling that goal will bring us. The problem is that feelings and emotions don't last. There is a distinct difference between an emotion and an emotional state.

The trouble in chasing an emotion is that what you're chasing isn't really there. Every time you think you've reached that feeling, you'll have to reach it again, and again. Now you may be saying, "Well, yeah. I want to be happy over and over again." But the issue is when you put value in that single emotion and not in your state of emotion. We are going to talk about state much more as we go on, but I want you to see the flaw in this concept so that you can clearly understand your goals. Take buying the dream home as an example. It would be hard to argue that buying a dream home wouldn't bring you joy and happiness, but what about after you buy it. What happens in ten years or even two years after the purchase? Is that home bringing you the same level of joy it did the first day you put the key in the door? That emotion of buying the home is most likely long gone by now. So, now what? What purchase or possession do you chase now? You have to find another achievement to accomplish in order to feel that joy, to feel that happiness. What if you reshape that goal to seek a state of emotion and not a single emotion? Instead of wanting to buy a dream home, pursue a place to build a life in and fill it with memories of family and love. That state of emotion has longevity and it requires growth in achievements and accomplishments that will only build on its certainty.

Now, I am sure you will hear people preach about goals and success all the time, especially in today's social media world of entrepreneurs. "On that grind; chasing dreams; hustle all day," are just some of the comments I see every single day. Don't get talking about hard work confused with setting appropriate goals that might actually lead to some. Be careful of what it is that you are actually chasing. Are you looking for achievement, for acknowledgment, or for fulfillment? The ultimate goal should be fulfillment. We are going to get into pretty deep concepts of fulfillment later in this book but look at yourself right now. Are you fulfilled? Reverse your thought process and chase the end state. Go after the results and not the means that you think will get you there. If your goal is to provide for your family and to be a loving person to your spouse and children, then set your goals for that and not for the objects or possessions that you think will make you that person. When you properly align your goals with what you truly want deep inside, as you look to fulfill your life, you will see that the achievements just come along the way. The emotions you once sought after are now what fulfills your daily life. Objects, possessions, or finances are all just milestones of your real aspirations. **Seek for your soul to fulfill your life, and not for things in your life to fill your soul.**

O   O   O

So, keep that in mind as we move into this first exercise. Remember what real goals sound like and feel like. Don't limit yourself to surface goals. Don't fall for feel goals. Look deep into your soul, connect with yourself at your very core, and see that person. What does that person look like? Be honest with yourself about what it is you really want because I want you to take some time and write down three goals, in three specific areas of your life. You are going to write down the most prominent three things you want to happen in each area of health, relationships, and business. I don't want you to jot down bullet points. I want you to take a moment, close your eyes, and envision yourself and your life with these goals accomplished. I want you to really focus here. This is where you really see yourself. I want you to envision these goals at a time when you've accomplished them and step into that moment. I want you to be exhilarated about where you see your life. I want you to experience the joy and excitement of how those achievements make you feel, and then I want you to write them down in that state of mind. Ready? Set. Go! Yes, go now.

(A notes section has been provided in the back of this book for you to utilize.)

You should have nine solid goals before you that add some real value to your life. If you don't think they are perfect, or you're struggling to find ones in a certain area, that's okay. Just like our values tend to shift over time, so will your goals. Life's ongoing changes will bring about new and different aspirations. New relationships, children, or career paths, all can have a different set of goals that come with them. As you reach and achieve certain ones, you may need to create new ones to continue to grow and succeed. What you'll find by the end of this process is how much it will apply to all aspects and ambitions of your life. You can revisit and refine them as often as you see fit, but you must identify them with the same process and write them down in the same manner.

The reasoning associated with the specific manner of writing out your goals and ambitions isn't just to post them on the fridge. It's because we are biologically visual creatures and we need to see a tangible goal in front of us for it to truly resonate. Research conducted at Dominican University in California showed that writing down goals enhances goal achievement. You may have heard of Harvard or Yale studies done on graduating business classes, but I have to inform you that those studies are just an urban legend. The study mentioned in California though actually set out to prove that myth accurate and did so in scholarly fashion. It shouldn't take a Ph.D. to understand that writing something down comes with a higher degree of commitment. I know word is bond, but a signed contract sure does make me feel better. The neuropsychological effects associated with thinking, saying, and writing down specific goals with visualization and emotional attachment, is a valuable tool to utilize. Our brain is broken up into multiple regions that are each responsible for different kinds of information. The more that an idea or piece of information can be processed and connected through multiple regions, the more likely we are to give focus and commit it to memory.

So, making adjustments to your goals is encouraged, but ensure you use the same process. Demand more than surface goals. Altering and refining them is perfectly ok because the ones you've written down are real. Do this with confidence, because your goals are not some random number associated with achievement. A random number that carries no real emotional connection to what you truly want out of yourself. It can be easy to give up on a number or to adjust it to fit what you've already done. However, no one will go from "I want my children to be proud of me" to, "I want my children to think I'm about average." That is the reasoning behind creating goals that have real fulfillment with what you truly want out of life. So, take something like, get a raise or promotion and change it to –

seek more responsibility to provide more financial security for my family. With each goal, ask yourself what it is that you genuinely want to come from it. How will it truly impact your life and what it will mean to you when you achieve it? Then, rewrite that goal to reflect its true purpose. You have now shifted from a set of goals to a defined purpose.

Do not underestimate the power of purpose. Certain things in life, you have to be pushed into, and others pull you in. Purpose pulls! It pulls you out of bed in the morning. It drives you to live for that purpose; it is something you can even be defined by. No one wants to be defined as the big guy who lost 50 pounds, but I bet they wouldn't mind being dubbed as the role model to their children. **Purpose is powerful.** Purpose can provide certainty. Certainty is the foundation of our beliefs. That belief is an important aspect in fulfilling your newly defined purpose. You don't need to know how you are going to achieve it yet. You just need to understand and believe with absolute certainty that you will.

Nothing happens until the pain of remaining the same outweighs the pain of change.

— Arthur Burt

People often describe how it took them years to change when in reality the change happened in an instant. It may have taken years to come to that instant, but the actual change happened in the blink of an eye. A decision was made. A point where change became the only avenue available. With absolute certainty, a decision was made that life was going to change and current behavior and beliefs could no longer exist. Take solitude in that understanding. Society and culture have lead us to believe that change takes time. No, change is in but an instant. It is in your absolute certainty. This is why I explained to you that where you're at right now doesn't really matter, but only where you want to be. As you close your eyes and connect with your ambitions, it provides you with the greatest picture of who and where you are, in your soul. Believe in it, for that is who you truly are.

O   O   O

As I said before, throughout this book we're going to focus on health and fitness; then you can take these same principles and apply them to other areas of your life as well. The reason I focus on health is its incredible relation to all other parts of life. You will come to find that it is the catalyst to all your ambitions. No matter the purpose, your health will be the foundation to propel you into it. The foundation, the ground floor you should build everything else upon. Your health and fitness level goes far beyond vanity or a number on a scale. The simplest forms of commitment, confidence, and discipline, all start with the ability to take care of yourself. Increased energy, improved memory and cognitive function, better sleep, the release of feel-good chemicals to improve your mood, are just some of the benefits of daily exercise. In the next few chapters, I'll be explaining it all, and you're going to appreciate the psychological impact that exercise really comes with. You'll understand the effects, and how to capitalize on them as they spill over into other areas of life.

So, to move forward, I want to take the health goals you have created and carefully examine them. You should have some refined purpose driven statements. Some goals and ambitions that truly resonate with you on a deeper and emotional level. I want you to look at each one individually and now think about the impact that it will have not on you this time, but on those around you. What will it mean to your spouse, to your family, or to your friends? What kind of impact will it have on those closest to you? Think of the attraction and intimacy you will bring back to a relationship. The energy levels you will bring to parenting or your family. The example you will be to those around you. What do you think it would mean for you to accomplish these goals, to the ones you love and care for the most? Take a few moments and really bring that feeling to the center. Then write down what you think that looks like, or feels like for each one of your goals.

There is one last step in this writing process. This final aspect of each goal that you have listed is a tangible one. Up to this point, you have taken your ambitions and defined them for a purpose and attached your emotions and the impact they have on those around you to each one. Now, I want you to attach a few dreams to your statements. Think of this as the proverbial bucket list of your initial goal. What would be an amazing experience that you could have when this goal is achieved or in the process of doing so. Odds are, you've probably already thought of a few things when we were visualizing the excitement and experiences associated with each goal. This can be anything, I mean anything, you want it to be. Think big! This could be taking up a hobby or sport with a loved one, participating in a fitness event or competition, doing a swimsuit photo shoot for your spouse, finally participating in something you've been unable to do, or a number of other things. The focus is to list something that you would either never have the confidence to do, or simply couldn't do physically prior to fulfilling your purpose goal. Here are a few examples:

- Snowboarding/Surfing
- Skydiving/Rock Climbing
- Marathon/Tough Mudder
- Local Sports Leagues
- Fitness Competitions
- Hiking/Adventuring

I want you to think big in this task, but remember it just has to be big to you. Don't discredit something that may have a considerable impact on your life, because it may not seem that big to someone else. I have had clients come to me with some heartbreaking stories and experiences. Tough ones, like standing in the long line of an amusement park ride with their children, only to finally get to the front, and not be able to fit in the seat. Then having their children turned away as well, because they need an adult to ride with them. The public embarrassment of that situation, only to be compounded with the disappointment and embarrassment of your children is painful to listen to. Even more agonizing to experience, but if you have had similar experiences or issues, this is not the time to shy away from them. This is the time to liberate your soul from any traumatic event you may have had to endure. Whether it was with your health and fitness, your finances, or any area that you may have had a brutal experience, you can turn it into a positive one instead.

I've stood in the grocery store checkout line and not had enough money to pay for everything there. Standing with a line of waiting people looking on, staring at bags of groceries, and knowing you have to go through the embarrassing and awkward moment of saying you need to put something back. Moments like that, of humiliating hardship, can be cruel but they can be eye-opening as well. Turn that incident into a motivational tool, rather than a painful memory. Take that time, harness that experience, and know that it will never be something you will encounter again. Know it with certainty! Know it in your mind and in your heart as you decide your own outcome. Write that event down in the way it will unfold this time around. Remember this is the dream bucket list of your goals, but it can be as simple as ride a roller coaster with your children. Doesn't seem to be that big, but in retrospect of the previous circumstances, that is a pretty profound statement and a tremendously rewarding goal.

O   O   O

Now, let's take a look at what we've accomplished thus far in this chapter. We will take a quick review of each aspect of the process, the reasoning behind each one, and provide you a clear picture of the foundation you've established. First, you've taken your original ambitions that may have just been surface goals and given them real depth. You've built a meaningful and emotional attachment to each one. This has given you the ability to connect with yourself regarding what you truly desire. These are no longer simple goals, but your purpose-driven aspirations. Understand that! The statements you have written are the purpose behind your ambitions. Do not lose sight of that.

One of the ways to ensure that doesn't happen is the reasoning behind the second step in the process. The meaning your goals will have on the ones you love and the ones you hold closest to you is no longer an afterthought. It is now at the forefront of your understanding. You wrote down the positive impact each goal would have on them and that is something you now have to be willing to abandon before giving up on yourself. Failure is no longer an option that will only affect you. The last item is the dream bucket of your goals. It's there to serve you as a tangible pinnacle of your achievements. It is something you can grab hold of. It is not the reasoning in your purpose, but a mere mark of accomplishment. It is the traditional light at the end of the tunnel, a victory dance for your soul.

As you close this chapter, remember the *how* is not important, only the *why*. You should have a precise picture of why in your mind and in your heart. You fully understand the power of the mind, the implication of every thought, and the reasoning to cultivate your thinking. Everything you have poured out onto paper is real. With absolute certainty, you can move forward. In but an instant, the changes have already been made. Now, we begin to put change into action!

CHAPTER 3

CREATING CHANGE

However beautiful the strategy, you should occasionally look at the results.

— Winston Churchill

Change is a word that can frighten most of us, even if it was one we needed to hear. We are habitual creatures who find comfort and solitude in what we already know. What we love, is certainty. Certainty of particular expectations and outcomes. Certainty of who and what we think we are. We tend to fear what we do not know. We fall into the arms of our comfort zone, where we perceive our control to be, whether we have any or not. We, as humans, have a tendency to become complacent in our lives. We become content in our current surrounding whether good or bad. We resist change or even deny that it is possible. This is why there are entire career fields for this in business, with change management and change consultants. We refute the acceptance, or possibility, to a point experts in the process are needed.

Resistance to change wouldn't be such an issue if the majority of us were actually satisfied with where our lives currently are. However, recent polls indicate that only 33% of Americans view themselves as happy or fulfilled with their present lives. You must ask yourself why would someone who doesn't feel happy, or even content in their current life, be so content living in it. The answer is certainty. Our roots are so firmly planted in certainty, that we would rather live a life unfulfilled than one uncertain. Think about that for a second. We would prefer to live certainly unhappy and unfulfilled than uncertainly happy and full of joy. Knowing and understanding that will be the insight to the three S's that lie ahead.

○   ○   ○

State, Story, and Strategy. The only three things that you ever have to consider when wanting to implement change. These are the keys to a breakthrough. Unfortunately, we usually only focus on one. Guess which one? When we do come to a point in our life that we feel change is needed, we tend to immediately look for a strategy to make it happen. What we usually ask ourselves is "what do I need to do to make this work?" We are all guilty of this because quite honestly, it's the most logical perspective. Something isn't right and we are looking for a way to fix it. The right strategy can save you valuable time in your approach. It could save you years, money, and a lot of wasted effort.

So, what is the right strategy? First and foremost, copy what has been proven to work. Find someone who is successful and mirror what they do. There is no shame in the plagiarism of life. In fact, I encourage it. Don't try and reinvent things where someone else has already done all the trial and error for you. Take a proven plan and run with it. Sometimes, someone else's strategy may not always work for you, and that's okay. Strategies are everywhere you look. Sometimes to a point where it's almost an overwhelming amount. Look at the fitness industry and the millions of diet plans, training programs, and so-called experts at every corner. High protein, vegan, gluten-free, carbs are good, carbs are bad, healthy fats, low fat, timing, macros, calories, aghhh! You want to pull your hair out; I get it. Let's be honest though, is it really that hard to get into shape?

It's not some secret only the wealthy are privy to. It isn't restricted to some elite membership. There is a fitness center, a book, a video, or an app available everywhere you turn. The information is there, and it's really quite simple. Then why does our society struggle so much with health and weight-loss? One is because people are often looking for the quick solution, or magic pill to fix all their problems, but that's not the real issue.

The real issue that arises is what if the problem is not the strategy? Haven't we all heard that one person say that they have tried everything and nothing works? How many times has that person been yourself? I hear this all the time in the fitness industry and it usually is in reference to diets. I hear, "I have tried thousands of plans and none of them work." When I ask for them to name them, they usually can only name a few at best. We went from thousands to two or three. That's a slight bit of a difference. What most of them have done, is tried the same two or three things thousands of times. Take a look at that for a moment. Repeatedly attempting the same plan, again and again, ending with the same results, but somehow expecting something different. That's the definition of insanity, but we wouldn't view it as insane. We would merely see a flaw in the strategy as the main reason why failure happened yet again.

See, we tend to think that the correct plan (strategy) will create a change in us resulting in a new or different life (story). Then that new life will bring us true joy and happiness (state). The right strategy will change my story and improve my state. What if I told you that logic was completely backward and the reason for ineffective change? What if I showed you that your state would change your story? That with the right state and the right story, the right strategy will present itself? That's the real key here, and to be honest, the part that really screws with your mind. Understanding that the key to change isn't about how to change, is a hard one to swallow. That certainty that we live in, that's our story. That's our belief system. It has a subconscious control in what we do and how we do it. That story has the greatest impact on our state than any other aspect

33

of life. We will live in it, good or bad because it's the pages of our book, completely unaware that we are the authors.

It reminds me of the story of an alcoholic man saying, "I will stop drinking when life gets better," not realizing that life would get better if he would stop drinking. Even in this example, the suggestion is that a simple strategy to quit drinking would change everything and make life better. See, the strategy of not drinking isn't the issue. It's the story of how bad his life is. It's his certainty. That certainty then alters his state. If you've ever seen addiction, you would know perfectly well that a simple strategy to quit, is not the answer. That is why just about every recovery program focuses on controlling thoughts and behaviors first. The same reason I emphasize on mindset instead of diet plans with my clients. To see this, you don't have to be an addict in its truest form. Quite honestly, we are all kind of addicted to our own certainty, to our own story. The strategy is usually never the issue. Do you think with the right state of mind, the right energy, and the right story, that you could find the right strategy?

Divorce your story and marry the truth.

— Tony Robbins

I heard Tony Robbins explain once – when a child begins to walk for the first time, how often do they fail? How many times do they stumble, wobble, and come crashing to the floor? At what point do we as parents look at them and say, "okay you're done, you're never going to walk, you're just not a walker"? We don't! That's absurd, and one of the best analogies I've ever heard. The reason is that's not their story, and we know with certainty it isn't. We approach each and every time they attempt to do so in a peak state of excitement and anticipation for what we know will eventually happen. Now, imagine that same state and certainty when approaching your own goals.

State, what do we ultimately mean when referring to our state? By definition, state is a person's condition or attributes, a status or position, or even a person's condition of mind or feelings. So, when I discuss your state, I'm actually referring to all of them. I'm referring to your physical and emotional level in a current moment. Your state of health, state of mind, state of excitement, and state of emotion. These are all factors in the process of change, but don't confuse a single emotion with an emotional state. As we briefly touched on before, a state of happiness is not the same as a time of feeling happy. Your state is the bigger picture. Your state is a vital part of your ability to learn and to perform. It affects your ability to complete tasks and analyze problems. It's an important aspect of your daily life, and all of it plays a critical role in creating a *Relentless State of Mind*.

Have you ever played sports or watched a football game? Ever seen a huddle of players before they take the field, jumping up and down in unison, shouting and chanting at each other? They are changing their state. Tapping into that energy, they need to perform at the highest levels. Can you imagine if you could get a group of high school students to do that, in the same manner, to prepare for an algebra class? How well do you think you would have done in college if you reached a peak state prior to every lecture and exam? Your *State* is a game changer. When beginning anything, and I mean anything, ask yourself if you're in the right state to complete the task. If you're not, get yourself there first. *Change your State – Change your Story!*

Your story. The certainty you've come to love and understand or loathe and expect. Either way, it's certain. It's what we as humans tend to long for, even if that certainty is variety. See, your story doesn't always mean the same thing; it may just mean the same outcome. That's what it was for me, and it caused a great deal of hardship in my life for quite some time. Your story is what you've come to know as true. Your truths are ultimately your beliefs. Think of someone's beliefs,

35

or even of your own. None of us are going to be persuaded from our own belief systems easily. Neither will we want to vary from our own story. *This always happens to me – I never win anything – I will never find love – I'm always overlooked.* These are just a few examples of beliefs taken from people's stories. Some look at these as just mere statements of frustration, but they are much more than that. They are beliefs, limiting beliefs, and they're not always verbalized. Many times, these beliefs lie below the surface or even in the subconscious. They are the stories you tell yourself. The reasoning and excuses you bring to the table. It's ultimately the story of how you see yourself, and **your story will become your reality.**

More often than not, many of our stories are limited by aspects beyond our control. Things other people have done or are being done to us. Particular environments or other factors become our reasoning we find ourselves in certain situations. Our boss, our spouse, our parents, the economy, the government, are all the blame for how we feel, for how we see ourselves. You then become just another character in your story rather than the leading role. Your story becomes the focus of everything else but you. **Where focus goes, energy flows.** The key is to bring the focus back to yourself. To understand that you are the author of your story and can write it however you see fit. If you're unsure of how your story looks, go back one chapter. That's you. That is the story you wrote when you solely focused on you and the person you envisioned at your very core.

Changing your state doesn't always mean jumping up and down like a football player to get yourself amped up to take on the world. Although it never hurts, it isn't always required. I don't expect you to head-butt your cubicle wall, repeatedly shouting "bring it on!", before you enter every office meeting. That would be pretty awesome though. What it does mean, is focusing your energy where it needs to go. Putting energy into things you can control. Taking responsibility for your actions and your emotions. There is no other greater example than that of Nelson Mandela. Wrongfully imprisoned in South Africa for 27 years of his life, he emerged a stronger, more distinguished, more refined, and more composed man than when he entered. He is widely known for exiting the gates of prison without bitterness, publicly forgiving his captors, and unifying a segregated South Africa as the first democratic President.

Forgiveness liberates the soul, it removes fear…

— Nelson Mandela

We can learn so much from a man like Nelson Mandela, but what I want you to take away from this, is his understanding of focusing his energy on the things he could control. If anyone had the right to lay down and blame everyone else for their problems and suffering, it was he. If you study his time in prison though, you will see that was never his outlook. He altered his state to reflect his story and not his circumstances. He was a leader of his people, an educated man, well spoken, well dressed, and composed. Even in filthy prison clothes doing manual labor, this is the man he portrayed. Do not let circumstances define you. Let your soul be your definition. All too often we are altered by one of two things, anger or fear, if not both. Both have the ability to consume us and alter our state. It is up to you to focus your energy, change your state, and not allow those debilitating emotions to take control of your story.

When you find yourself in that state, that state of depression or frustration in your current situation, you must ask yourself where your energy is flowing. It is flowing wherever you are focusing. Those two emotions, anger and fear, are most likely the underlying causes. You're angry at your circumstances, or fearful of your situation. You have anger for those who wronged you, or afraid of your outcome. Whatever it may be, you must reassert yourself. Change your state. The moment you focus on you, on the story you wrote, you can change your physiology in an instant. You sit a little straighter, walk a little taller, and smile a little longer. Those enervating emotions cannot exist at the same time in an altered and heightened state. Just like Nelson Mandela, you can alter your state regardless of circumstance.

○   ○   ○

How does knowing all this help in changing your state in order to change your story? It allows you to see the patterns that we create for ourselves, our set of beliefs, which are certain and are hard changed if compartmentalized in our minds. Remember the brain is always looking for patterns. You must create a new pattern to provide a new story. Just as we discussed before with writing down our goals, we want to do the same when introducing something new into our minds. We want to do so, into multiple different regions of the brain, in different compartments and components that are responsible for different functions. When you change your state and you vocalize it, envision it, truly stepping into that moment, and feeling the emotions it carries, you're connecting all those properties of the mind and committing them to memory. You're rewiring your computer to see the patterns of your own reality.

The reason identifying these patterns we create are so important is in the instances when changing your state only affects the surface. Do you recall when I explained to you that your certainty didn't always have to mean the same story, that it sometimes just meant the same outcome? This was my particular circumstance. I understood how to change my state; I had been doing it my entire adult life. It was something that the Marine Corps had instilled in all of us, knowingly or not. As a leader of Marines, you must present yourself as the quiet professional at all times. Regardless of the ensuing chaos, you must demonstrate composure, act with integrity, and display unwavering amounts of character. The task at hand is irrelevant to the level of enthusiasm that should be displayed while completing it. There is a comical saying in the Marines, that even false motivation is still motivation. This is essentially changing your state, but only your physiology. However effective for training and completing tasks, it isn't going to change your state at the core. This is why tapping into every aspect of the mind that you can is so imperative. Understanding the patterns, you set for yourself, will guide you to the changes that need to be made.

For me, it wasn't my peak state but my end state. I had already prewritten the final chapters to my story. These were certainties I had built from my past and stored in my mental hard drive. I had determined long ago that certain things in my life would never be attainable, things I didn't deserve, and aspects of life I shouldn't have the joy to experience. I fully accepted this and understood it with absolute certainty. I call this the "state of acceptance." This was my story, and as one should expect, my story most certainly became my reality. I continued to lead by example, always having myself in a peak state, and attacking the day in a relentless manner. I adopted a life of trying to help others and bring as much joy as I could to those around me, in almost a sick sort of redemption for my own history. All while secretly knowing inside, that I would never live a life of real joy and fulfillment.

I changed my state every morning when I woke, attacked the day in true military fashion, and then returned to my own picture of existence. I had conditioned myself to do so from the day I stepped onto those yellow footprints at just 17 years of age. Years later that change of state wouldn't matter. I was so certain of my story and my outcome that I would go through all sorts of destructive behavior. Finances, relationships, friendships, all took a beating for years. None of it was ever really the same, but all of it ended in the same outcome. I wasn't going to allow myself to build a family, build financial security, build healthy relationships, or have any real fulfilling joy in life. Why? None of that fit into my story. Those things would have shattered my beliefs, the things I was certain of in my life. That my life was to be one of hardships, struggles, and the constant battle with the demons of my past.

During that time in my life, I didn't understand the difference between an emotion and an emotional state. I would rise every morning and think aloud that I have the choice to be happy or sad today. I would loudly proclaim that I was going to be happy. Thinking that for some reason just saying it would make it true. I was proud of the simplicity I had created. That life was just choices, and this was just another among them. I was completely lost. So many of us live in that public happiness and come home to our own private misery. I was chasing a single emotion every day, and doing it with positive thinking. It took me quite some time to realize the error in that concept. I don't want you to make that same mistake.

I want you to understand that in some cases, false motivation is still motivation, but not when addressing your personal story. I operated every day in a false sense of a peak state. My state was a mask to my story. I needed to change my story. How did I learn to do that? Well, there are a couple of unique factors, and some we will address later, but I want you to leave this chapter knowing how important your purpose is. See, I altered my state in order to lead, to work, to perform, never was it for me to live. I never laid out my goals and envisioned myself as the person I was in my very soul. If I had done that, and altered my state to step into that moment, I would have never been able to stay in the story I had created. Take that to heart, and look at the patterns you've created in your life. What is the common denominator? Are you attempting to change your state to match your purpose? Do you see yourself in that moment? Can you feel the emotion and the impact it has on you and those closest to you? Do that, change that state, and you will truly rewrite your story!

The strategy you now seek will be clear. You are no longer looking for the strategy that will change your story. **You're looking for a strategy that supports your story.** With the right state, things inside of you begin to shift. When you have a purpose, your disposition changes. I'm going to share with you a fitness industry secret that most professionals won't want you to hear. I have met quite a few people over the years that have lost massive amounts of weight and made some pretty amazing transformations. I don't mean my clients. I mean people who have made these huge changes all on their own. When I asked them about the plan they used or the program they were following, they all had the same exact answer, "I'm not."

They had NO strategy! They had no plan in the sense of a diet, or a program, or some other guide, to show them the path to change. They didn't use a magic pill or wrap, or some other infomercial product to achieve it either. When I asked, "So, what was it you did? What changed?" They all replied the same exact way, "I did." They changed! They all in their own words would describe how they just started eating healthier, started exercising, and made sure they were accountable. That's it. No secret potion, no secret plan, nothing. The strategy they used is one they didn't even know they were using. They all had done their own research, they removed things from their life that were holding them back, and they made a commitment to themselves and others. That so-called "strategy" presented itself because they had changed their state. That change in state completely changed their story. All of them told me in one way or another that they had had enough, and the person they saw in the mirror wasn't the person they saw in themselves.

Doesn't that sound pretty familiar to everything you just read? They saw a different person in their soul then what they saw in the mirror. They changed their state to reflect that person inside and not the reflection in front of them. Right then, their story changed. No longer did diets *not work*, no longer would

41

they fail. The strategy didn't really matter anymore because they were going to do whatever it took to fulfill the person they truly were inside. When that happened, everything they needed to do just presented itself. Why? Now, they were actually ready to look for it. They were ready to hear it. They were all ready to find it, and find it they did.

O   O   O

One of the biggest factors as to why things just begin to present themselves is your reticular activating system or RAS. The RAS is a bundle of nerves at that base of the brain that controls different aspects of how we receive information. Your brain is actually far more powerful than any computer in its ability to process data. It has millions of bits of data coming in at any given moment. The issue is that we simply can't comprehend that amount of information and our brain knows that. So, the RAS filters out all the information our brain takes in and brings only certain things into our conscious mind. It basically acts as a filter to what we deem important. What *we* deem important. Meaning, you have the control to adjust that filter, to adjust your RAS. It works like this. Have you ever bought a car or an outfit and then began to see that car or outfit everywhere you went? It's not that the car and outfit were never there before, it was that you just didn't notice them. There was now a level of importance associated with them, and your RAS allowed that information through to your conscious mind.

Now, you may have been told that this is the law of attraction, where what you think about will become reality. It's often referred to as the powers of the universe, and this external force that is interacting with the energy we put out. Nothing could be further from the truth. It is completely internal and biological. I want you to understand that, what this really is, is a neurological response. I explained to you from the very beginning that your thoughts will mold your surroundings. It is not in the universe; it is in you. It's the perfect nature of our unique design. What you see and feel internally, will be manifested in your consciousness. The term higher consciousness is accurate, but its reasoning usually isn't. What a higher level of awareness or consciousness really is, is understanding how to control the filter to your conscious mind. Your thoughts will alter you minds filter, your RAS. This is why controlling your thoughts is so important. This is why your state and story is so imperative because you can't lie to your RAS. This is the awareness.

Do you want to know what the law of attraction really is? It's when optimistic preparation meets opportunity. That's it. When you set your sights on something and start to work towards it with diligence and enthusiasm, you actually begin doing things that will bring you closer to achieving it. Imagine that? Crazy, right? You change your state to an energetic and positive approach to whatever it is you set out to achieve. Your RAS starts to deem things associated with that goal more important than it did before. So, next time you're in line at that coffee shop and you over hear a conversation that you may not have noticed before, not only are you aware of it, you're ready for it. Preparation meets opportunity. Pair that with optimism, focused energy, and a positive attitude, and you will see those around you respond. That's not the universe, that's you!

When all those individuals changed their state, and their entire story began to change, their reticular activating system did as well. The information around them that they weren't aware of before, all of a sudden came to them. The right strategy just began to present itself. As we move forward, I'm going to give you the formal blueprint of what all those people did on their own to lose the weight and change their lives, but understand that the correct strategy was never their issue with weight. The story they had regarding their weight was. The moment that shifted, everything else followed suit. I cannot emphasize that enough, how important that shift needs to happen before anything else.

Throughout the next few chapters you will begin to build your tactical approach to success in health, as well as every other part of your life. However, you have to be the one ready to find it.

CHAPTER 4

PURGE, PREPARE, PRIME

I am not a product of my circumstances.
I am a product of my decisions.

— Stephen R. Covey

In combat operations, we continually analyze and assess our course of action (COA), and that of our enemy as well. What is the avenue we are most likely to take? What is the enemy's most probable COA? Does this make operational sense and are there mitigating factors? These questions pose real threats that need to be considered, evaluated, and possibly resolved. This approach is also essential to life's operations. The actions we take in pursuing the life we want needs to be analyzed and determined if it's the best course. We need to look at the enemy of our dreams as well, ourselves. What is the most probable action we will take to hinder our own success? How often have we traveled down this same road to no avail?

In this chapter, we will discuss in detail that same combat methodology and the application of how to *Purge, Prepare, & Prime.* First and foremost, these are the most regimented steps in the *Relentless* process. As I've mentioned before, information is just an understanding and holds no real value until that knowledge is met with action, and not just any action, but massive action. Understanding and applying the information in this chapter will set the entire process into motion. It is simplistic in its design, yet sometimes difficult in its execution. This can also make these steps feel daunting during the process. Up until now, we have talked a lot about our thoughts, looked at our mental process, and did a few exercises on paper. Now it is time for a course of action, and purging your life is real in-your-face kind of action, that can be hard to stomach. It means breaking bonds, trashing items, and emptying the storage closet. It's clearing the stage so that you can prepare a new scene or in some cases a whole new show. Only then are you ready for priming! This is where we take all the information you previously wrote about yourself and introduce it to a massive course of action.

The Purge - Well, not exactly like the blockbuster title but pretty damn close. It's time to throw on a mask, grab the proverbial baseball bat, and get ready to smash some stuff. We are going to go step by step through the exercises you did earlier, discarding everything in your path that does not directly support or serve your purpose. Understand that this can have two astounding and completely polar opposite effects on the psyche. You can let this process be draining and difficult to bear or exciting and liberating in nature. The choice is yours, but I'm a fan of the latter. It's a mindset shift from the word "go," and you're going to get there by changing your state before you begin each step. Remember, no amount of training or planning will help you execute if you haven't conditioned the mind to be in the proper state during execution. It's a mindset. So here we go, time to trash, delete, block, and rid your life of a lot of things, I'm sure at one point you thought you could never live without.

We are going to continue to focus on health and fitness and the written exercises you did in the previous chapter. Recent clinical studies revealed that less than 3% of Americans live a healthy lifestyle. So, I can assure you that whatever your health and fitness goals are, you most likely need a serious overhaul to properly align them with your purpose. The mind, along with the body, requires fuel to function, generate, rebuild, and recover every single day. For both of them to operate at peak performance, they require a performance fuel. You require a performance fuel. No different than your mind, regarding thoughts and information, is your body in terms of stimulus and nutrition. Good seed will reap a good harvest, just as poor seed will reap a poor one. What you consume in your daily nutrition will consume you in your daily life. In the simplest of terms; If you eat garbage, you will look and feel like garbage.

I am sure that you have heard sayings and taglines of – *Nutrition is 90% of The Game – Abs are made in the Kitchen – You can't out train a bad diet,* and on and on. Well, those statements are true, yet normally followed with a faulty approach. No matter your genetic makeup, physical nature, or athleticism, chances are you've been on a diet of some sort and just as likely, more than one. Weight loss is a $60 billion-dollar industry with more than 75 million Americans attempting a diet at any given time, with more than 80% of them failing to keep the weight off long term. Now, is that because the diet wasn't effective, the nutrition was confusing, the plan too expensive, or maybe just too difficult to follow? Odds are, none of those reasons had anything to do with the success, or lack thereof, in any of those diets. Again, the focus was on the strategy, a diet or plan with no regard to state or story. Where was their mindset? You should probably be picking up by now that I'm not going to guide you through any dietary strategy either.

I am not going to tell you what to eat, how to eat, or when to eat it. None of that truly matters in terms of success in your daily nutrition. Instead, I am going to attack your common sense and your kitchen pantry in a relentless manner, that demands you take responsibility for your own mind, your own body, and your own life. No longer will petty excuses and lack of information be tolerated as a viable explanation to poor nutritional habits. I have heard just about every excuse over the past decade, and I can honestly say that probably less than 3% of those excuses actually carried some weight to them. I'm not talking about – *I just don't know what to eat* – *I don't have enough time* – *I thought that was healthy*. I mean real issues that severely impact someone's effort in managing their nutrition, like having a child with an immunodeficiency disorder that requires constant attention and living in and out of hospitals every single day, or like someone who is trying to raise four children by themselves while living below the poverty line and working more than 18 hours a day. Those were some pretty demanding circumstances, but even they could accomplish things with the right state of mind.

State of mind is where we will begin before each and every step. The state in which you approach your transformation is key to your follow through, to your relentlessness. So, before you begin any step, get yourself excited for an incredible change. Think of the massive success you'll have and envision your life the way you want to see it. With a determined focus, an elevated heart rate, and a clear mind, it's time to *Purge*! We are going to begin with the fuel you put into your body. You are going to go through your entire kitchen and remove every single item. Yes, every single item. Lay them all out on the counter, table or even the floor. You must remove everything to understand and visualize the number of items you actually have. Once you have removed everything, you may then begin to put things back one by one, as you eliminate everything you know is not healthy for you. I mean everything! You're not going to eat it, or donate it, or give it to friends and family; you're going to trash it. It is a liberating and meaningful experience to see the amount of food you must purge from your life to even start. Embrace it!

You are an intelligent person and I can assure you, deep down you know what is healthy and what is not. You are a determined person, and you're not going to let doubt deter you from this process. If you think it might be unhealthy, it is! You want to clear the stage for you to prepare a new scene. Odds are, if it's in a box and has a paragraph of ingredients, it isn't good for you, and it has to go. Leave no corner or cupboard unchecked, no refrigerator uncleaned, everything must go. Remember this is a step in a change of mental state, and the process is more important than the ingredients. Now get up, get excited, and Go!

We started with nutrition because it sets the tempo, it's a simple decision-making process that provides an immediate response. Not only is the nutrition-step an integral part of your mental state and wellbeing, but it becomes a catalyst in the purging process. It represents the true essence of the task, which is to remove everything that has outlived its purpose and is no longer in alignment with your current goals. To see the trash bag(s) of things that have been holding you back is important to see. It is important to clear things out as a whole to understand them in their entirety. Do not attempt to purge items or areas in your life in sections or portions. Concerning nutrition, this is the concept of cutting out one bad dietary choice at a time. I'm sure you've seen nutrition plans or diets that talk about removing one item at a time and reaching little milestones along the way. This is a classic sign of a strategy focus, someone who has not made any change in state and is undoubtedly stuck in the same story.

This type of plan exists, because it is a belief that a plan that removes everything is entirely too difficult. It is a *belief*. That certainty we long for. Remember the limiting stories – *Diets never work for me*. So, we devise a plan that limits our commitment and lowers our expectations. No one goes on a diet, continuing to make poor choices, and truly believes that they will achieve an ideal outcome. So, when failure arises again for them, it was actually just an underlying expectation. Then yet again, the story is confirmed for them, that diets never work. *Certainty*. Ah, but then there are the diet plans that don't slowly make limitations and are an all-in process, right? These highly marketed diets usually have an extremely short shelf life though. I'm referring to the infamous 60-day challenges, the one-month makeovers, and the week-long juice cleanses. Changing your nutritional habits for a few weeks didn't create any new habits. Your mind, your state, all knew it was going to be over soon. Then what? What did you actually change? A temporary strategy was implemented for a long-term goal. If you knew someone was dying from lung cancer, would you advise them to cut back to just a few cigarettes a day? Or maybe you could just get them to quit smoking for a month or two? That sounds absurd, doesn't it? It should because it is.

This is why you need to purge items as a whole so that you can see things in their entirety. You need to understand the things that are adversely affecting your purpose. You need to evaluate each one. When you can look at things in your life based on purpose and not on their individuality, immediate progress can be made. **This is when the shoulds, become musts.** We all have things we should do – *I should eat better, I should exercise more, I should quit smoking*. Not until those statements turn from should to must, do you honestly make a change. That must, comes from your purpose.

Remember when I explained to you how people change in an instant? Well, I started smoking in high school. Like so many others I knew at that age in the 90's, it was just cool to do. It was a part of the bad boy image I thought I wanted at the time. When I joined the Marine Corps at 17 years old, it was almost a part of our culture to be a young, combat-hardened warrior. I smoked nearly 15 years straight, trying to quit a few times along the way and always knowing deep down I *should*. It wasn't until I started in the fitness industry with a real passion for helping others, that I just up one day and quit. It no longer aligned with the image I had of myself. It didn't fit my purpose. How was I going to help and advise people on their health and fitness when I was damaging my body every single day? I knew right then, I *must* quit, and without a second thought, I did. For years I attempted to quit, and then in one single moment, I changed in an instant. Nothing was ever going to change until that habit no longer aligned with the person I truly was on the inside. Until it was no longer how I viewed myself.

Make sure everything we begin to go through is evaluated for how it stacks up to the person you really are. It is very important to see that. You must physically touch tangible items and personally write down all those that are not. Focus on each individual item and its value in your life. It doesn't have to serve a direct purpose in your goals, but it cannot hinder them in any way. Any and all things that impede change and your progress must go! To make big changes, you have to make a significant leap, so take bold actions.

Now that you have a purged kitchen and a solid understanding of the process, it's time to continue on to the next step. We are still focusing on your health goals and the clear purpose that you've defined. What you're going to do now, is to begin to list all the things that you know will hinder your purpose, limit your progress, and deter you from the changes you've already consciously made. Anything and everything you can think of that has caused you to derail in the past. Things that have caused you to procrastinate in taking action. Anything that has caused you to doubt yourself. Things you know will be issues when you begin to change, and anything you can think of that might become a roadblock in the path ahead. Don't overly evaluate anything as of now, just write down everything that comes to mind. Go on a rant in your list, blurt out anything you can think of, and then write it down. Remember to get yourself into a peak state, envision those changes, get excited about the work you're doing. Then write in that manner, in that state. Here are some areas to consider when making your list. These are common areas in us all that need to be evaluated and purged.

- television and movies,
- social media and videos
- games and mobile app
- unsupportive friends

- excessive nightlife
- obstructing habits
- alcohol, tobacco, drugs
- addictive behaviors

Be as honest as you possibly can here. Personal relationships can be a very difficult area to explore. However, you must really ask yourself what environments are you putting yourself in on a daily basis that are not conducive to your purpose. I find it mindboggling sometimes when I hear people's stories and then evaluate their environments and relationships. Probably the number one reason I hear for failure to exercise and eat properly is time. People continuously tell me they just don't have enough time in their day to accomplish these extra tasks. You know that very well may be true, which is why we need to purge our lives to create physical and mental space for things that truly serve our purpose. However, I would ask clients all the time if they had a favorite TV show or what their social media habits were. Almost everyone would discuss them with me and we would analyze that a minimum of three to four hours a day were spent on television and just mindlessly scrolling through social media feeds. Hours and hours a day essentially spent doing nothing, but in their story, in their belief, they had no time.

I was even blown away at myself when I looked back and analyzed how smoking didn't just impact my health, which was more than enough to make a change, but how much time I had wasted. I would on average lose over two hours a day just standing around smoking, sometimes even more. I would have to stop what I was doing, head outside or away from where I was, and lose all momentum on the task I was working on, just to fulfill a ten-minute fix. Every single day. What things do you do in your life that have the same time consuming, stalling effect, on your daily progress?

What about environments and people? It's heartbreaking to watch someone want to make a change, begin taking some steps, and then falter because the ones they tend to associate with pull them right back into the very behavior they are trying to change. You wouldn't recommend an alcoholic to hang out at a bar or associate with other drinkers. So, why then would you put yourself in situations or in the company of people who directly hinder your vision and purpose? Look at your social settings, the people in your life closest to you, that you know will have an influence or impact on your decisions, behavior, and overall purpose. If you can see areas that may pose a problem, you must take action. This can be difficult to do when you begin to think of family and friends, and those you are loyal to. I tell my clients all the time that they need to be prepared for the ones they love the most to become the first ones to create obstacles in their journey.

You know why strangers support you more than people you know? Because, people that know you have a tough time accepting you come from the same place while they are still in the same place.

— Unknown

Some of your closest friends and family will be the ones questioning your motives, deterring you from your goals, and placing doubt in your new beliefs. Most of the time, this isn't a malicious attack on you as a person, but a defense of their own certainty. Your commitment to change will bring about specific changes in the lives of those closest to you. That means things they were once certain of, will no longer be. When you begin to make positive changes, especially with your health and fitness, it consequently causes those around you to question their own lifestyle and choices. This doesn't sit well with many people and it can be followed by some pretty harsh criticism. I have heard the terms obsessed, anal, delusional, vein, dysmorphia, and more, all as reasoning to why healthy choices are being made. I always found it amusing to see how up in arms people would get about someone else beginning to make healthy decisions in their life, but yet never batted an eye when that person sat around stuffing their face with pizza and ice cream. It will seem that everyone will have an opinion when you begin to make changes in your life, especially ones for the better.

Sometimes, especially with the ones closest to you, your own expectations can cause the divide in your relationship. Not everyone will hold the same enthusiasm that you do for the changes you're making, and not everyone has to. Don't be unsettled if people close to you don't share your motivation. Some will be defending their life choices to themselves, others will ridicule you for yours, and some will simply be indifferent. Be careful when you realize this pattern amongst some of your closest friends and family, for they are the ones you need to evaluate the most. It's evident to most of us that we wouldn't keep a person in our life that sat around telling us we will always fail, and to give up because we are worthless. I want you to be able to see that the person that keeps you from your goals, grounded in their certainty, and dismissing all your aspirations as misguided fantasies, is in no way any different than the other person. They both want you to give up on your dreams; one just masks it in a blanket of friendship.

Reevaluate the aspects we just discussed and confirm you've listed out everything you can think of. As you formulate the list of areas that need to be limited or completely removed from your life, you're ready to take some big actions. Next to each item on your list, you're going to write an action item. An action item may be as simple as tossing out a gaming console, deleting an app, or canceling a subscription. It can also be more difficult in ending unwanted friendships, having strong conversations with difficult family members, or quitting an addictive behavior. All are equally necessary and should excite you to take action. Remember the change has already been made, you are now just putting things into motion. Any action item you write down that can be completed immediately, do it right then and there. If you're addicted to an app and spend hours a day playing *Candy Crush* on your phone, I will assume you listed it as an item to purge. The action item of deleting that app is immediate. The moment you write something like that down, do it. There is no reason to delay that action, pull out your phone and delete the app. For those action items that are a process, or may take some time, make sure you do something now to initiate them.

You may delay, but time will not.

— Benjamin Franklin

As you begin to progress in your daily changes, you may begin to see some of the behaviors I was describing, in your friends and family. In the event of that becoming an issue, sit down and begin the writing process over again, evaluate the areas or people that need to be addressed, and take serious action! When starting this process in other areas of your life, do something similar to the nutrition step, that's immediate and initiates the process. Just like we started with the kitchen and purging all the food we no longer needed in our lives, find a similar area that can be an immediate area of action. These act as a catalyst to the overall process and commit you to change. Then continue on, list out all the things that pose a threat to your purpose, and write out action items that can be made to mitigate or eliminate those threats.

I'm telling you if you just learn to accomplish the principles up to this point you will be wildly successful. You could stop reading right now and see amazing results in your life just by what you've done up till now. You have attacked this with military precision. You created a mission with a clear defined purpose of where you want to see yourself. You know it with certainty, with absolute certainty. You know it's not in some amazing strategy because just as in combat, no plan survives the first contact with the enemy. The change lies within your story and you know the way to an amazing story is in a peak state! In the right state, the right strategy will eventually present itself. Just as in battle, you have identified the items that pose a threat to your operation. You have systematically analyzed and mitigated any aspects that may prevent you from your goals, from your aspirations, and from your true purpose. You are already a warrior. **You are already Relentless!**

O   O   O

To Prepare – You are already well ahead of the game, but to begin to execute at the highest levels, you must prepare. To begin to prepare, you must look closely at the task and purpose you are preparing for. One does not take up knitting to prepare for war. You purged your life to create physical and mental space for certain items, relationships, and understanding that bring real value to your goals and purpose. Now is the time you begin to prepare those areas to be filled. Here is where we create the specific tangibles. I had you redefine your goals so that you could clearly see the purpose behind them. Now we need to create specifics.

Just like you made a list of items to purge that would inhibit your purpose, you are going to make a list of action items that will support your purpose. I would like you to address each goal individually and write down at least two action items that are necessities to fulfilling each one. These are the items we discussed earlier that have moved from shoulds to musts. List items that will have a specific impact on your life and purpose. As you evaluate each goal and list your action items, there are three main aspects to consider – *Availability, Accessibility, and Accountability.* In a bit of wordplay on the financial world, I like to call these AAA Bonds. If you can confirm all three A's, you can guarantee a solid return on your investment. What you're looking for, is this:

- Does this work within my current schedule?
- Do I have the resources to make this happen?
- What have I done to commit myself to the action?

With each action item you create, you're going to want to answer these questions and then provide necessary solutions. To get yourself started, it's often a simple practice to list the item that coincides with what you've purged. Remember we cleared out physical and mental space in the previous exercise to clear the stage. Here is where you build your new set. You're creating the scene that now fits your purpose and showcases the person you truly are. If you listed – *No more Fast Food during lunch breaks*, then you'll need to fill that void with something else. That may look as simple as – *Prepare and Pack my own lunch every day*. However, this may require an additional action item, like – *Learn how to cook*. You're not listing things you should give up or change from your daily habits. We are listing the things that we need to add to our life, items that will lead to our success.

Many of your action items won't necessarily fit with an item you purged but are an obvious requirement to fulfill your goals. Take an exercise program for example. Exercise must be a part of your daily regimen; there is no room for compromise here. So, you have to ask yourself, do you have time in your schedule available for daily exercise? What things or habits did you clear from your day to provide that availability? Do you have enough resources to exercise? This can be a number of things, from a corporate fitness facility to a couple of dumbbells and a jog around the block. This may mean you need to consult a professional, buy a couple of books, or do some research on the internet. The central theme here is, do you have access to a form of exercise? Then finally, what have you done to make yourself accountable? What steps did you take to become committed to the action? Maybe you signed a yearlong gym contract, hired a personal trainer, or invested in some in-home gym equipment. These are all great actions of commitment, but nothing has greater accountability than a public declaration. This could be an open post on social media, telling all your friends and family, or a simple text to the right person. A person who can be stern and hold you accountable is a valuable resource, and I highly recommend seeking someone out who can fill this role for you.

This is how you prepare. These are the steps you need to implement in preparation for the purpose you have outlined for yourself. These are the specifics of your purpose, the tangibles of your goals. Apply these same principles to other areas of your life, outside of health and fitness, and prepare in the same manner. List those action items associated with each goal and then run them against your rating system. Are you Available? Are they Accessible? Are you Accountable? If not, take the necessary measures to make it so. Ensure your goals have been rated AAA so that you can guarantee a return on your investment.

Availability + Accessibility + Accountability = Attainability

In preparation, you must reach a certain level of commitment. In terms of life and battle, there is no other phrase more rooted in commitment than "Burn the Boats." A literal order given by some iconic commanders to burn (or to scuttle) the ships they had arrived in, in order to eliminate an avenue of escape. This was done so that when they entered into battle, there was no available retreat. There was but one path, and it ended in victory or death. Majority of the time this was done when armies were drastically outnumbered and a mental commitment needed to be achieved prior to entering what appeared to be a suicidal mission. Now, you may think this is a little extreme for a health and fitness goal or any goal for that matter, but it's these actions of commitment we are after. It is the thoughts associated with no retreat, the mindset of determination, and the power of the mind to continue during any adversity. When I ask you to take an action that commits you, I want you to **Burn the Boats!**

The Marines are known to be able to do more with less. When compared to the other armed forces, the Marines always seem to be underfunded, understaffed, and with outdated gear and equipment. We seem to revel in it though, that no matter the insurmountable odds, we will be victorious. There is a saying we have that embodies this spirit, "improvise, adapt, overcome." Simply stated, that no matter the circumstances, plans will change, you need to adjust, and still accomplish your mission. The Marines are known to be highly resourceful, which is a skill you need to personify. Failure is usually accompanied with a list of things people didn't have. They have no time, no money, no support team, no this, or no that. What I end up hearing, is not a lack of resources, but a lack of resourcefulness. So, when you begin to evaluate your own accessibility, remember to **improvise, adapt, and overcome.**

We've discussed the influence of writing things down and how it impacts our focus. You've written out goals and purpose, and you've written out specific action items to help you achieve them, but what about the day to day operations of life? We're all wired the same and there are certain chemicals in the brain that will dictate our actions. Dopamine is a neurotransmitter that helps control our brain's reward and pleasure centers. It enables us, not only to see rewards, but to take action to move toward them. This is one of the simple reasons behind writing tasks down, and why it feels so good to check something off as we accomplish it, no matter how small. It's those little hits of dopamine. Now, dopamine plays a complex role in our mesolimbic pathway, but you often hear it discussed with just pleasure and addiction. That's all well and true, except the part I want you to understand, is the focus. Dopamine is released when we see something we associate with reward, and will then cause us to focus more intently on that particular reward. This is extremely important in understanding our visual needs of tangible goals, how we focus on them, and how to exploit the reward center of our brains in their achievement.

A great tool to use for this, and one that is probably the simplest form of self-accountability, is a date calendar and Jerry Seinfeld's infamous – *Don't break the Chain!* The premise is a natural exploitation of how our brains work at the most basic level. The plan works like this. Have a standard date calendar in the office, on the fridge, or someplace that will be highly visible to you. Every day that you work towards your goal, or complete your specified tasks, you make an X in that date block. It doesn't matter what you do, or how you do it, just as long as you do something. This is about accountability, not execution. As you work toward your goals, you begin to make a chain of X's that will look more and more gratifying as the days go on. The day you don't work towards that goal, you don't get to place an X in the date, and the chain is broken. Que Jerry, "Don't break the chain!" You now have to start over and make a new chain. This works well with specifics that aren't thought of in too broad of terms. For example, exercise is a great "Seinfeld Strategy" type of task. Every day that you work out, you get an X – *Dopamine*. Every day you don't, you don't.

These two daily tips are great tools because they work off our brains release of certain chemicals, which are biological driving factors of certain actions. Making lists and checking them off, releases those chemicals. Looking at the next item on the list releases dopamine that causes us to focus on completing it, just so we can cross it off. Simple, almost comical, but true. When we associate pleasure or rewards with a particular object, just seeing that object can influence us. Eating is emotional because we get a release of dopamine when we eat something like cheesecake. By just seeing cheesecake, we get a release of dopamine, because we associate it with pleasure. That causes us to focus on the cake in efforts to receive that perceived pleasure. Just by seeing it, we feel good. Just by seeing it, we focus on it.

O   O   O

Prime In – As a Marine Corps Assault Breacher, I was tasked with gaining access to enclosures through dynamic entry. In other words, I blew up doors to make a SWAT-style entry into buildings. A pretty cool job, I must admit. With every explosive charge I built, it required a system to set it off. This system is referred to as a priming system. No matter the number of explosives, or how elaborate in design I made each charge, it still had to be primed. To prime: to prepare or make ready for a particular purpose or operation. This is the last phase, to make you ready for igniting a significant change in your life. The priming systems I used in explosive breaching is conceptually no different than the priming systems we're going to use here. You're going to use priming to initiate an explosive response to gain access to your real purpose.

Understanding priming from a psychological standpoint is actually quite simple, and it's where you get to play mind games with yourself. Priming is where you use a stimulus to generate an implicit memory effect to influence a later stimulus. Basically, using visual and auditory cues to generate the desired response. It works like this. I show you one thing, so your mind can quickly access or associate it with another thing I show you later. Hold a cup of hot coffee in your hands, and the person you meet in the coffee shop may seem to have a warmer personality. Pretty crazy, right? Well, it can get pretty interesting. Research has shown all kinds of different effects priming has had on the human psyche and I'm going to show you how to take it to new levels and implement it into your daily living.

There are studies that have shown when a group of test subjects were primed with a list of words that were associated with the elderly, prior to taking a test, the outcome of the test had no significant change. Yet, everyone leaving the testing site walked out slower than the control group did. That was the real test. Just being shown words that were associated with being old, made them move and walk slower. There is also research that shows polling sites will influence a voter's ballot. When a polling site is at a school, voters are more likely to vote for tax increases to support education. Visual exposure to a sports drink increased participants physical output in another study.

Think about that for a second, just showing someone a sports drink can make them work harder.

This works psychologically in a number of ways and has numerous different aspects and theories of its implementation. Simply explained, we are going to prime your brain so that it is more in tune with the defined purpose you have established. Some may say that priming yourself is just creating little reminders for yourself throughout the day. Reminders are sticky notes on your computer or alarms on your phone to complete certain tasks. Priming is about creating these subtle cues of association, which generate a subconscious response, even when you're aware of their presence. Just like an actual primer, you're laying down a base coat so that things will stick.

Understanding how your mind associates certain stimulus with thought is the key to priming. I've explained how the brain is compartmentalized with different regions that are responsible for various functions and information. The more we get information to pass through multiple regions the greater chance we have of committing that information to memory. That data is then stored in schemas (units) in long-term memory. The more these schemas are activated, the more the information becomes available to the conscious mind. The more you can get particular schemas to activate together will cause them to create bonds with one another. It creates a brain network of stored information. Priming is how we increase the accessibility to these schemas of information. It's the way we rewire our brains so that we have a desired thought process that is in line with our desired outcome.

To be yourself in a world that is constantly trying to make you something else is the greatest accomplishment.

— Ralph Waldo Emerson

Here's an example of how this works in scientific research. If I were to show you pictures of yellow objects and then asked you to tell me the name of a fruit, your response would most likely be a banana. Being the most common fruit associated with that color. Now, if I showed you pictures of red objects, what do you think your response would be? Yeah, most likely you would respond with an apple. This is a form of priming in its simplest form, and something you may see in a specific kind of study. So, how does priming work in everyday life? Believe it or not, you are constantly being primed. If you walked past a phone and remembered to call your mother, you've just been primed. The phone made your mind access information associated with phones, like making phone calls. That information triggered a response in associated schemas and accessed information previously stored in memory, like calling your mother. We are being primed all the time, by all sorts of stimulus that's around us. Many times, that priming has an effect on us that causes thought patterns we really don't want. Like walking past that box of donuts in the office and then making poor lunch choices later in the day. Now, it would require so much energy and attention to fight the effects of priming, that I wouldn't even attempt to try. What we are going to do though, is be the number one source of the priming in our lives.

There are different types of priming regarding psychology, such as associative, semantic, conceptual, positive, and more. I highly encourage you to read up on it more, as it is a fascinating subject of the human mind. For our purpose, we are going to initially be focusing on a dual, repetitive and semantic, concept of priming. The concept we are going to use is really quite simple. We are going to prime your environment with ques that trigger associated behavior and thought patterns in a manner that allows the highest volume of exposure to those ques.

When we look at the semantic field of our health and fitness goals, we want to try and focus on the things that will create an implicit memory effect related to those goals. For example, when we think of healthy eating, we may envision fruits and vegetables, the words organic or gluten-free, or even terms like whole foods. All these things will cause an implicit memory effect of healthy eating when primed. What about exercise? Do you see weights and a gym, or think of running and track shoes? Maybe a yoga mat or water bottle? All these things have a priming effect on the human mind. By utilizing this process, we are going to ingrain the desired behavior we want at the cognitive forefront of our minds. We are going to fill all that empty space you created with the positive primers of your new purpose.

The best approach here is to give you some examples that you can implement in your life in order to prime yourself for a healthier lifestyle. I'll provide you with a list of actions that can be taken and the implicit memory effect that can be derived from them. Priming common focal points in your home or place of business is an easy start. This is attacking areas that you spend ample amounts of time in. A good example is centerpieces and baskets of fresh fruits and vegetables, that can be on the kitchen counter, the dining room table, atop the office mini-fridge, or desk at work. Real or fake doesn't matter, it's the visual cue you're after to create that association with eating better. Coffee tables and end tables get magazines and books associated with healthy living and exercise. You don't even have to read them; it's just the implicit memory effect you're after. Water bottles on the kitchen counter, in the front of the fridge, on your desk, or in your work environment will prime you for hydration and limit the want for unhealthy beverages.

Emplacing deliberate visual ques for daily living, are specific items strategically placed to prime regular activities. A set of dumbbells, yoga mat, or exercise ball in a corner of your home. You don't have to use these items; you may workout out a gym, but it's the repetitive priming of exercise you're looking for. A gym membership tag attached to your keys for the office or car. A packed gym bag that sits in the passenger seat, with water, gym towel, and any needed equipment. Again, I don't care if you use that bag or not, it's the response that bag will initiate. Gym clothes laid out at the foot of the bed or the back of a chair, running shoes placed by the front door, or a fitness book by the TV remote. Repetition, repetition, repetition.

You need to begin filtering media and information sources to better align with your lifestyle. You want to manage your garden, and allow the right seeds to be planted in your daily living. Changing your social media feeds to healthy living and fitness associated pages and personalities. Platforms like Facebook, Instagram, and YouTube, are filled with information and inspiration for healthy living. Change what the internet is trying to prime you with. When you search for a particular item, ever notice that item now pops up in ads all over the internet for you? That's because most web pages use intelligent ad sources, and that directly responds to your recent internet searches. So, search healthy eating, exercise, running, and anything else associated with healthy living. Not so you actually respond to the ads and purchase items, but so that you are being primed for health and fitness every time you're on the web.

Auditory priming is a great resource to use at some point in the day and can come in many forms. Most of us tend to listen to music throughout the day at certain given times. Switch some of those moments to motivational speeches, audio books, or even a podcast on health and fitness or any other topic associated with your goals. Listen to them while driving to work, while going for your run, at the gym, when cleaning the house, or in your morning routine. Even when not fully engaged, and just using it as background noise, you'll subliminally pick up the messages within the content. It's the message you're after in all these examples. The information your brain receives that you may not even notice, and then stores in memory, will affect your later thoughts.

We've gone into some great detail about priming and its effects, and we are going to discuss some deeper areas of priming in the next chapter. I've explained it in such a manner because there is no real way for me to guide you through priming steps on your own individual goals. Therefore, you need to have a clear and concise concept of what priming is, and how to effectively implement it into your life. I've shown you numerous examples of how to prime for health and fitness, but you will really need to apply the concept itself to your other goals. Look at the associative qualities of the primers we use for fitness and how that might look in other areas of your life. Finally, take a step back and see how this third step brings the whole process full circle.

The three P's of this chapter are essential. They are the very backbone of change, but I want you to understand a valuable point here. I want you to recall the individuals I told you about, the ones that had made these significant health changes all on their own. The ones that said they had no strategy, the ones that just changed. In conversation, almost all of them told me how they quit all the BS that was holding them back. Some told me about how they started reading more about health and fitness, and two were even inspired to get personal training certifications for themselves. They **Purged** their lives of the things that no longer fit with the person they knew they were inside. They then began to **Prepare** themselves for the life they were certain was theirs. That life then became filled with things associated with their story, like exercise equipment, athletic apparel, healthy foods and supplements, books and magazines, and even social media feeds. All of those things were around them all the time. They **Primed** themselves every single day, whether they realized it or not.

The ultimate strategy in *Purge, Prepare, Prime*, is that there isn't one. Tap into that person who you found in previous chapters, the one you see in your very soul. That person knows with certainty what they want out of life. That person already knows what to do.

CHAPTER 5

ROUTINE, RITUAL, RELIGION

If you want to make your dreams come true, the first thing you have to do is wake up.

— J. M. Power

Morning routines are a common practice in some of the world's most successful people. One of the more notable ones would be Tony Robbins, who often speaks of the ten-minute ritual he does every morning before starting his day. I have listened to Richard Branson (founder of Virgin Group), as well as Robert Iger (CEO of Disney), Jack Dorsey (Founder of Twitter), and many others discuss their individual morning routines. They all seem to have some sort of regimented structure to start their day. Some of the most influential and successful people in the world that are running multimillion, and even billion dollar companies, all have this methodical routine every single morning.

How is it, if you ask the top businessmen and women from around the world about what they do during their mornings, they all seem to have a similar answer? Is it some secret among the über elite, or is it one of the reasons that has actually contributed to their success? I'm sure you can answer that one. Their success can be contributed to many factors, but I can assure you they all have a deliberate routine with very precise reasoning. It prepares them. It primes their behavior. It serves their purpose!

O   O   O

Routine! Take a look at the routines of as many Fortune 500 CEOs as you'd like, and I guarantee in the majority of them, you will see some form of physical exercise first thing in the morning. It may be a walk with the dog, some cardio, a full workout, or just a quick bump in heart rate like my routine, but it's there. It was no secret in the military, of the positive effects a proper morning routine had on daily productivity. Reveille was sounded every morning at 0530 and was immediately followed by certain tasks and physical exercise. The common aspect of all of them is the physical priming taking place. We discussed priming and its effects on the human psyche in the previous chapter. Now, we are going to look at the process of physical priming and its impact on the human body. Remember the importance of your state in every exercise you did earlier? How state altered your manner in which you approached tasks? Well, physical priming is altering your physiology for what lies ahead. Just like a true primer, you're preparing yourself for the day.

By putting yourself through some sort of physical exertion each morning, you're priming your entire mind and body to execute tasks at a higher level of performance. Scientific research has shown in numerous different studies how physical activity improves cognition, particularly frontal lobe-mediated cognitive processes, such as planning, scheduling, inhibition, and working memory. That's right; exercise improves your ability to plan project tasks and efficiently schedule your day. A morning jog will improve your memory causing you to be more efficient and increase your productivity. Ah, but the big one is inhibition. Exercise can improve inhibition, the constraint in impulsive thoughts and behavior. Our thoughts, so much of who and what we are is derived from our thoughts. Something as simple as a quick morning exercise can curb some of those impulses and desires that creep into our day. One's that don't fit the person we truly are. One's we may continue to struggle with as we make changes. Exercise can help you manage the weeds.

Do you recall, when I asked you what it would be like if you could get a high school class pumped up like pro football players for an algebra class? It would be pretty amazing, right? The increases in attention spans and individual learning capacities would be unimaginable. Well, not anymore thanks to certain high schools that have adopted the process of physical priming into their education plans. These programs have added simple exercise protocols intended to increase students heart rates for at least 15 minutes each morning before heading to their academic classes. Without fail, every single program and study showed an increase in not just academic performance, but in executive function as well. Students received higher test marks, better grades, and noticed an increase in planning, organization, and self-control.

Why is this so important to understand? It's important because it's so vital and so often overlooked. It becomes one of those areas, where we know there are some benefits, but not to the extent that we truly understand its significance. Take the No Child Left Behind Act for example, a federal program in the United States designed to ensure students test at appropriate levels throughout their education. Due to the government's mandates and pressure of standardized tests, schools across the nation began cutting back on physical education and recess time for students. The thought that increased classroom time to focus on academic material would subsequently increase test performance. The exact opposite of what all research shows will happen when you eliminate exercise. As we continue to make more technological advancements, we tend to live more sedentary lifestyles as we go. If you look into the near future, we are literally setting up our children to perform at the lowest levels.

This applies in adulthood even more, because we tend to slow in cognition as we get older. Sedentary lifestyles are all too common these days, and our culture doesn't seem to be making any significant changes to remedy that. Consistent physical activity will reduce the cognitive decline associated with age. Did you catch that word there, consistent? Consistency is what transforms us. **Consistency is what builds habits**. Remember, we are habitual creatures with minds that are constantly looking for the patterns. The patterns we can consciously and consistently create for ourselves will become the habits of our life. We just have to create the right ones. The ones that support the life we have envisioned for ourselves.

Continuous improvement is better than delayed perfection.

— Mark Twain

The best way to create the right habits is by structuring routines that will allow you to build on consistent behavior. You may have heard that it takes 21 days to form a habit, but I have to inform you, that is the best-case scenario and not even likely when developing new habits. That figure came from *Psycho-Cybernetics* by Dr. Maltz back in 1960, and even he stated, "...that it requires a minimum of about 21 days for an old mental image to dissolve..." The minimum, not the standard. Other studies have shown that on average it takes 66 days to create a new habit. Here's the real answer, no one knows how long it's going to take to form a new habit. The data in those studies actually ranged from 18 days to more than 250. So, hey it could be three weeks or 8 months. The point is that it doesn't matter. You're creating routines of life, the time frame it takes to go from task to habit is irrelevant.

What should you look for in a morning routine? I like to think that my daily routine should be viewed as the *Example* for my life. *Exercise, Experience, and Excitement* should be the foundation of my habits. These three principles become what shapes my routine and ultimately guides me as life tends to shift over time. The first one, exercise, is the foundation of any morning routine. There is so much irrefutable evidence to the benefits of daily physical activity it has to be the basis of where you begin. You only need 10 to 15 minutes of increased heart rate, to reap the benefits of an early morning exercise program. When you attack the morning with that type of intensity, your body begins to release certain hormones that reduce stress, improve insulin function, and increase brain function and clarity. As if that's not enough, elevating your heart rate with intense exercise will rev up your metabolism and increase your caloric burn through excess post-exercise oxygen consumption (EPOC). The basic explanation here is when you hit it hard in the morning, you wake up everything in your mind and body that promotes better health and function.

This exercise routine can be whatever you would like it to be, as long as it's exercise. Weight training, cardio, yoga, or even something quick and intense are all great options. My exercise routine each morning is only about 10 minutes. I don't utilize my time in the morning as my primary fitness training, although I highly recommend it if committing to a fitness program is one of your concerns. To keep myself in good shape I utilize weight training, mixed martial arts, and other metabolic conditioning programs throughout the week. Even training as hard as I do, in and out of the gym, I understand how vital morning exercise is to my daily routine. So, without fail, like clockwork every morning, I get out of bed and head straight to the pool. I don't think. I don't dip my toe to test the water. I just dive right in.

In the mornings, even in Las Vegas, it's cold. That's a good thing. I swim as hard as I can for about 5 minutes, with a combination of strokes above and below the water. As the seasons change and it gets too cold to bear (usually under 50°F), I turn from swimming to cold water immersion. Cold water immersion is just a form of cryotherapy. Taking a cold-water plunge or even an ice-cold shower, if you don't have easy access to a pool, can reap some serious health benefits. Exposing your body to extreme cold will increase metabolism, reduce inflammation, as well as improve body hardening. Body hardening occurs when your body has to routinely adjust to rapid, low temperatures. This repeated exposure to stress increases your body's own tolerance to stress and disease. After years in the Marine Corps, and spending much time surfing off the coast of California, I have become quite accustomed to cold waters.

WARNING: When implementing cold water immersion into your morning routine, begin with a comfortable temperature, usually above 60°F. If you cannot regulate the temperature, ensure you are in a safe and controlled environment, such as a pool that you can safely stand up in. Loss of breathing control and intense cold shock is reached between 50 – 60°F. I do not recommend swimming in deep pools or open water until fully accustomed to your morning routine.

I then come flying out of that pool, wide-eyed and ready to go. I then finish my morning exercise routine with some sort of calisthenics. Similar to my days in the military, it may be 100 push-ups, crunches or lunges, stretching or a combination of similar exercises that will round out my morning of physical activity. This all takes me a little under ten minutes to complete. That's it, just ten minutes. So, instead of hitting the snooze button tomorrow morning, try hitting the cold shower instead. You will be amazed at how you feel renewed and completely energized for the day.

Once that part of my morning is complete, I head back into the house, looking to settle into an experience. What experiences do you value most? What do you enjoy most about your day? Is it family, is it friends, is it something higher? What part of life would you want to experience every single day? For me, I usually grabbed a cup a coffee and headed outside with my pit bulls. Watching them play in the yard and just using that time for self-reflection. Recently though, I have changed this part of my routine. Like I said before, life will tend to shift over time. As I write this chapter, my daughter is almost two weeks old. Now, she is the experience I long for. Watching her sleep, or grabbing her so that her mother can get some, is what lights my morning up. That's what you need to ask yourself, what will light up your morning?

This is where you build in the time, that will allow you to create these precious moments and experiences. The ones that we all tend to say pass us by all too quickly in our busy lives. Gary Vaynerchuk, who is notorious for planning his day down to the exact minute, calls his mom, dad, or sister every morning on his way to the office. He catches up on what's going on in their lives and just sees how they are doing. The mega-entrepreneur says he really values those small moments. Maybe for you, it's coffee with your spouse where you just talk about each other for a few minutes. No phones, no kids, no schedules, only the two of you, just a few minutes a day. Maybe you don't even need to speak at all, just being there next to one another is the experience. Maybe it's making breakfast with the little ones. Perhaps it's being alone with a chapter from the current book your reading. In my opinion, an experience doesn't always have to be this amazing once in a lifetime event. It can be common, right there in your kitchen, and carry so much impact on your daily life.

No matter the experience you choose to build into your morning routine, ensure it's solely for the experience. Point being that not one part of this routine involves your cell phone. None of it requires you to check your email, or look at the market's opening numbers, turn on the news, or check your social media feeds. It is about bettering you as an individual, through valued personal experience.

The last part of the routine is to create excitement. This is where you prime your mind to ignite your day. The two main factors in creating this aspect are to change your physiology and adjust your focus. Just like we have discussed over and over, you need to get yourself into the appropriate state before taking on any task, and that includes the tasks of daily life. You need to proactively and consciously get yourself in a peak state, and really focus the power of your mind. You're going to do this through a self-empowering ritual as a part of your morning routine.

O   O   O

Rituals. Many people confuse their routines with rituals. Unlike your morning routine, which has specific aspects but not specific actions, a ritual is a series of steps that are performed in a very prescribed order. Rituals are usually solemn in nature and serve a direct internal purpose. Think of meditation or a breathing exercise, done in a very specific manner. The benefit of the right ritual is hard to put into quantitative data, but I can assure you it has a profound and near philosophical effect.

So, what is the right type of ritual? The one I use is a method of self-priming. It's aligning your focus with your goals, with your purpose, and who you are at your core. Where focus goes, energy flows. The priming ritual I use every morning is that of Tony Robbins. I am a firm believer that if it's not broke, don't fix it. I don't need to reinvent the wheel in an area of focus that a man has been successful at for nearly 40 years. The best part, neither do you. So, I am going to explain to you the process that he has taught to millions of people over the years. Tony's 10-minute morning priming ritual will change your entire day, each and every day.

You're going to start the first three minutes with a breathing exercise that will center you and create focus. Place yourself in a calm, quiet setting free of distractions, and close your eyes. You can be seated or standing in this exercise; I personally prefer to sit. You're going to start with your arms held high above your head, hands open wide as you breathe in, and then pull them down, closing your hands as you forcefully exhale through your nose. Reach open hands back towards the sky as you breathe in, and then rapidly bring them back down as you forcefully exhale through your nose again. Continue this process for about 30 repetitions (30 seconds), and then stop. Place your hands on your lap or at your sides with palms up and keep your eyes closed, and just relax. Relax and just feel your body (about 30 seconds). Then hands back up to the sky and start your breathing again for a total of three sets, about three minutes (don't time yourself, be in the moment).

Continue to relax after your last set of breathing. Bring your hands to your chest and place them over your heart. Feel your heart, I mean truly feel it. Breathe it in. Feel gratitude for your heart and your life. Then I want you to find something in your life or a particular moment that you're grateful for. If you can't, think of something that you could be grateful for. Some moment, or thing that if you had to, you could see gratitude in it. Things or moments that you can truly express real appreciation for in your life. You need to envision it. You need to step into the moment, feel it in your soul, and feel the gratitude you have for it. Spend about a minute or so here, and just be grateful. Then I want you to find two more things or moments you can truly feel gratitude for. Spend another minute with each one, really connecting with each one. Try and fill your heart with as much gratitude as you can, for life, for family, friends, things you have been blessed with, or even just the sun on your face.

Then, in the last step, focus on three outcomes or results that you are really committed to. See yourself accomplishing them and step into those moments as well. Visualize the things you want to achieve and picture yourself with each one completed. Let the full emotion of those achievements set in. Envision the impact those accomplishments have on those around you as well. Feel the gratitude you have in those achievements. Be thankful for those moments. See those things with absolute certainty. I like to personally see one goal or task for the day, one for the near future, and one goal a little further out. Again, spend a minute on each one and truly envision yourself in those achievements. For me, each day will bring about a new goal, but the other two more distant goals remain a part of my ritual until they are fulfilled. I see it as an unfaltering approach to the outcomes I feel committed to. I want you to decide on whatever three goals truly inspire you. That may be three distant goals that you see over and over or daily tasks that motivate you each day.

As the end state to your morning routine, the 10-minute priming ritual will be an absolute game changer. This process eliminates two of our biggest emotions in life, fear, and anger. In that calm state with a focus of gratitude and relaxation, it's impossible to feel angry or fearful. By focusing on your goals, and bringing those things to the center of your mind just before you start the day, you're actually priming yourself to focus your energy in that direction throughout the day. It allows you to tap into your reticular activating system (RAS), and prime it with what you've deemed as relevant information, your aspirations, and your ambitions. You now know your outcome, you now know your purpose. All in all, that morning routine is only 30-45 minutes in duration. In that short amount of time you can completely and radically change the course of your day, and ultimately the course of your life.

O   O   O

Religion. It's hard to go through that morning priming ritual and not feel a sense of spirituality within it. Quite honestly, it is a very spiritual process. Now, you don't have to be religious or even spiritual for that priming exercise to work for you. In fact, regarding neurophysiology, neither hold any real bearing on priming. However, I feel there is a greater understanding of gratitude in the sense of spirituality, and a power far greater than ourselves. I would also be remiss if I didn't eventually disclose my own personal beliefs in this book. It would be unjust on my part to teach you how to train yourself for the appropriate mindset, and leave out one of the most crucial aspects. I can give you all the tools and information available to take massive action and create lasting change. I can help guide you with military precision to achieve great success, but I have to admit to you at some point, that there will still be an emptiness within you that can only be filled by one thing.

For by grace you have been saved through faith...

— Ephesians 2:8

Throughout this process, we have frequently discussed the concept of looking inside yourself and really understanding you. To truly define your goals well beyond aspirations, and put them into real purpose driven statements. I have repeatedly directed you to the pursuit of deep fulfillment, over chasing temporary achievements. That understanding of real fulfillment can ultimately bring you to the greatest understanding of your true purpose. This comes from the immense amount of one single emotion, gratitude. A level of gratitude that can only be assumed, when you can begin to fully comprehend the concept of grace. **God's grace, and your absolute purpose.** In the next chapter, I'm going to reveal to you the true measures of personal success.

MY DAILY MORNING ROUTINE

0630	*Wake* – I drink 16oz of water immediately upon waking, use the restroom, brush my teeth, and change to head to the pool.
0635	*Exercise* – I dive straight into the pool for 5 minutes of intense cold-water swimming, or cold-water immersion to kick start my morning.
0640	*Exercise* – I do 5 minutes of calisthenics and stretching to increase my heart rate and get the blood flowing after the cold-water plunge.
0645	*Experience* – I drink 16oz of cold water with 2oz of apple cider vinegar, grab myself a cup of coffee and let the dogs out for a few minutes.
0650	*Experience* – The best part of my morning is some Daddy-Daughter Time.
0700	*Excitement* – After such a jump start of energy and emotion, I spend a solid 10 minutes in the morning priming ritual to gain complete focus.
0710	*Begin* – Now, I'm ready to attack the day!

CHAPTER 6

GRACE, GRATITUDE, GIVING

Learn to be thankful for what you already have, while you pursue all that you want.

— Jim Rohn

L ook up into the sky and try to comprehend the infinite universe that lies beyond. I want you to try and picture yourself in an out of body experience sort of way. I want you to see yourself standing here on earth amidst that vast universe. Just you, all alone, amongst the thousands of other people you live near. Those near you, that are all just a small portion of the millions within our society. A society that helps make up the vast population of the world. All 7.5 billion of them and counting. Looking at earth from our universe billions of light years away, do you look small? Do you feel small? Do you see how insignificant we are in the grand scheme of things? I don't say this to upset you, or make you feel inferior, but to bring light to our minuscule existence. Life is so much larger than we can imagine. We live in the infinite and understand in the finite.

Now, I'm not trying to tell you about life beyond our galaxy; I'm talking about life beyond our death. See, the grace I spoke about before, comes from the understanding in that this world, this universe, owes you absolutely nothing. You were born not of your own will; you were then kept alive not of your own doing. You were to some degree, regardless of circumstance, nurtured, sheltered and cared for without burden. You received life. You received mercy. You received a gift. That gift is grace. I briefly touched on being grateful and expressing gratitude in your morning ritual. However, you will never truly be able to understand the gratitude I am referring to until you can fully comprehend the grace that you have received.

O   O   O

Grace – So, what is it? Have you ever experienced something good in life that you know wasn't really justified? Something or someone just poured out into your life and provided you something at a time when you just didn't deserve it? Some see this as luck, or karma, or even the powers to be within the universe. Most clients I talk with, usually don't have a problem understanding that aspect. That sometimes life provides us with certain things we really didn't see coming, things we just don't deserve. What if I told you that you don't even deserve life itself? Would you begin to take a different approach? See, that's the depths of grace. That's the magnitude of what I'm trying to express to you. That is the level of gratitude you must come to understand. That in all honesty, in that grand picture of the universe, we deserve absolutely nothing, not even the life we live. However, by the grace of a merciful and loving God, we do.

The remaining portion of Ephesians 2:8, quoted in the last chapter, is this – *For by grace you have been saved through faith. And this is not your own doing, it is the gift of God.* – Grace has been bestowed on us by our God and Savior. We have been given life through our faith in Jesus, but I want you to see that we didn't even do that part. The faith itself that we have in Jesus is also a gift from God. In all sense of the term, we deserve absolutely nothing! We are not even believers without God's grace. When you can begin to wrap your mind around the magnitude of that gift, you will only then begin to understand the level of gratitude and fulfillment I am referring to.

Fulfillment is what we should all be chasing beyond any simple ambitions. Wouldn't it be great to know that you don't even have to chase it? That understanding of fulfillment has been given to you as a gift by God. You have the ability, because of God's grace to accept in Jesus. That aspect is what makes this entire process shift to an entirely new level. Understanding your place in the infinite makes your life and work in the finite so much more enjoyable. Realizing your significance is an insurmountable advantage in the world of life, love, business, and finance. No longer will you view the things through the eyes of the world.

Now, as I have warned you many times through this book of things like positive thinking and the law of attraction, there is an even bigger warning I must give you. Material ministries is a real thing, and not what I am trying to express to you in this book. You will come across many so-called Christian Pastors discussing the benefits of salvation through the increase of possessions and finances. There is nothing more biblically inaccurate than this type of ministry, and those preaching it should be considered false teachers. No degree of faith is going to manifest itself into worldly possessions. Being a believer in Christ does not guarantee you a successful life, only an eternal one. That is all.

Whatever you do, do it for the glory of God.

— 1 Corinthians 10:31

This doesn't mean that just because you are a believer in Christ, you can't be successful, or financially wealthy, or pursue goals outside of God. What it does mean, is that those aspirations should never be what you seek as fulfillment. It means that those aspirations outside of God should still be for God. Years ago, when I was struggling with my faith, my father and I were talking while on a surfing trip on the island of Borneo. He was telling me "when you do things, do them for God; when you pursue things, pursue them for God." I'll be honest. I didn't truly comprehend what he was trying to say at that moment. I was still stuck in that story of what I thought my life should be, and thinking that God could save me wasn't a part of it. What he meant, and what I am telling you now, is this – *Pursue your life for the glory of God*. Every goal, every aspiration, should be pursued with that thought at the forefront of your mind and soul. He told me on that trip just before I paddled out one day, "Today when you surf, surf for God." While out there on the water, it started to make sense. Looking at the most amazing sunset out across the water, off the shore of this incredible island, there I was, this small insignificant creature in this vast universe created by him. I surfed that day with the pleasure of knowing that all of it, the island, the waves, my ability to ride this piece of fiberglass across the water, all came from God. It filled my heart that day, the way no wave ever had before. They say surfing is spiritual. Yes, it is, but then isn't everything?

Those goals, which you created before, that we defined into a real purpose for yourself, I want you to take a look at them again. Understand, that those goals and your pursuit of them can be done for the glory of God. You can pursue each purpose with a relentless vigor because you take solitude in what you know as your true ultimate purpose. Which is to be a follower of Christ, to be a believer in our Lord and Savior. That will be the true measurement of your success, and the only real way to complete fulfillment. Your daily living in the finite is filled with peace because you have certainty in the infinite. Certainty, remember that word we long for in our lives. Nothing is more certain than knowing you're saved by grace alone, through faith alone, in Christ alone.

O   O   O

Gratitude – It is the undeniable emotion that results in the understanding of such grace. Now, you may not be a believer in Jesus Christ, and I fully understand that. Although I urge you to seek your own salvation, I still want you to understand that grace is still ever present in your life. You're here, you're alive, and regardless of circumstance, you're thriving. You may have a different set of beliefs, a different outlook, or maybe, you've never even given it much thought, but grace is still a part of your life. Why? How? At the most rudimental level of understanding, you're still here. You have somehow survived up to this very moment in time. Something you didn't necessarily deserve. The gratitude of you simply just being, is something to take refuge in. Gratitude is something you should find yourself in, each and every day, regardless if your reasoning differs from that of mine.

Look at some of the most successful men and women in the world, and you will see many of them talk about the immense amount of gratitude they have in their daily lives. Most of them also have a moment to focus on that area, as a part of their daily routines as well. You may say, "well, of course, they have so much to be grateful for." However, their successes are usually not what they have the deepest gratitude for, and most will say that they've had this understanding long before they were ever successful. They're not just grateful for their successes, nor were the only grateful after becoming successful. This doesn't mean that their success was a result of their gratitude either. As with all of the other warnings I have given you, here lies yet another. The attitude of gratitude, or the theory of thanking your way to success, has undoubtedly zero understanding, or any concept of real gratitude. The *power of gratitude* approach to personal success is an undeniable indication of a complete lack of comprehension. Gratitude has nothing to do with personal success and everything to do with personal fulfillment.

The power of gratitude, or thanking your way to success, is a misguided practice at its very best. Its intentions are solely rooted in self-attainment, and therefore hold no real value or understanding of gratitude. That sort of approach isn't really appreciative for what you have; it's a false act of thanks for what you think it might bring. To feel gratitude within the goals you envision yourself achieving, is still a good practice. However, only if you would feel that same level of gratitude if you didn't achieve them as well. To be grateful for even having the life and opportunity to attempt to pursue those goals is a real selfless understanding.

Gratitude is a powerful emotion and understanding. Without it, no amount of success will ever make you feel whole. How often have you seen someone with unbelievable amounts of success, with financial wealth that most of us can't even comprehend, and yet they still live in and out of rehab? People who seem to be on top of the world, yet secretly living in states of deep and dark depression. We look at those with immense amounts of wealth, and say, "What could they possibly be struggling with?" We think they couldn't possibly know any real hardships, because they can buy whatever they want. *Money can't buy happiness* – is not just a cliché. It's a truth, and it's hard for some to stomach that truth.

We must use those cases as examples to a greater understanding of what real fulfillment truly is. Success doesn't lie in material possessions, nor in wealth or status. History has proven that to us. Hollywood has all but sealed it into the walk of fame for us. There are so many different people we could reference that seem to have had it all, but battled with addiction, anxiety, depression, and even suicide. How is it, that someone who appears to have all the success in the world, be at a point so miserable, that they choose to take their own life?

To begin to understand certain behaviors, you must begin to understand your needs, the needs every human inherently has within them. Abraham Maslow developed a hierarchy of human needs that look at the most basic needs of existence needing to be filled before we can focus on more emotional and spiritual needs. Conceptually sound, but a crude approach to particular aspects, as he lumps certain physical and emotional needs together into categories. Tony Robbins lists six human needs that we all try to meet on some level. He lists the first four as emotional needs: certainty, uncertainty or variety, significance, and love and connection. These are our fundamental needs, needs we will instinctively find a way to meet. As I have said throughout this book, certainty is a big factor in our existence. We must have a degree of certainty even to begin to function. That is a part of our prewired survival instincts. There are particular areas of life that we need to be certain about. Ultimately as an assurance to avoid pain and feel some sort of comfort. There are many different ways to achieve this, but no matter the circumstance, we will find a way to do so. The problem is that we can reach an evident level of certainty in our life that everything becomes highly predictable; we get bored. When we are certain of every outcome, every response, everything in our daily life, we alienate one of our other needs, uncertainty. If we have no uncertainty in our lives, we're without variety. We miss out on the spice of life.

Those first two are divergent emotional needs that must find a balance within our daily lives. Too much uncertainty and we can reach a level of stress beyond our control. Too much certainty in our lives and we can become depressed and complacent. We have to create foundations in our lives that create a sense of certainty while giving ourselves occasional and adventurous variety with a bit of excitement. We can fill both those needs in a positive, neutral, or negative way. You could take a spontaneous vacation or have an adulterous love affair, and both will provide a level of variety and uncertainty. Meeting these human needs doesn't always mean it will add value to your life.

The next two also work in tandem as we seek significance we tend to lose connection. Each of us wants to be distinctive or important on some level. We want to be unique in our own way. We can find significance in a number of ways, through style, through beliefs, through success, or even through tearing other people down. All can give us the sense of being significant. As I referenced before, with particular Hollywood stars or those that seemed to have everything, their unique significance pulled them further and further away from any real connection. The saying, "it's lonely at the top" is very true. We all need some feeling of significance, a way to stand out and be exceptional in our own right, but we also seek love and connection with others, a sense of belonging. Many times, we seek connection because love can leave us vulnerable to being hurt. Either way, we still yearn for that sense of intimate interaction. However, the deeper we tip to one side of the scale, the greater the sense of loss is in the opposite emotion. These first four needs of the personality, drive our behaviors and will be met in one way or another.

As we take a good look at ourselves, we will find that our behaviors are just a response to trying to meet one of these requirements, if not all of them. We all have these necessities; we may just value each one a little differently. Every one of us has our own order in which we place these needs, and these are needs. These aren't goals or aspirations. These are needs that are inherent to every human being. There are positive and negative approaches to meet each one. How we go about meeting them, is intrinsic to our own beliefs and values. They are all too often met in terms of immediate gratification and hold little thought on our long-term quality of life. No matter our abilities to satisfy these instinctual requirements, we will never truly feel fulfilled. Not until we can learn to meet the final two, growth and contribution, will we feel a sense of fulfillment.

We can meet all four of our fundamental needs, and not experience any real joy or positivity in our lives. You can get certainty through anger and violence. You can get uncertain outcomes and variety through gambling or alcohol. You can ridicule people online to instantly feel more significant. In order to have some sort of connection, you can create constant problems in your life for people to be there for you. None of this makes you a better person or brings you any real joy, but meets every one of your needs. That's why we need to try and reach those needs through avenues that will direct us towards the final two more spiritual needs we have. We must grow, and we must contribute to something outside of ourselves. Unlike the needs of our personality which we will all find a way to meet, these are the needs of our spirit. This is what moves us inside, and not everyone will meet these needs, and ultimately never reach any real fulfillment.

Certainty – Uncertainty/Variety

Significance – Love/Connection

Growth – Contribution

Without growth, we die. For anything to continue, it needs to grow. If your relationship isn't growing, it will eventually end. If your business isn't growing, it will eventually go under. If we don't grow, we aren't really living. The moment we cease to grow, we begin to fade away. So, we can get busy living, or we can get busy dying. To live, we need to continue to grow and develop in physicality, in knowledge, and in our understanding. When that growth stops, subsequently so do we. Growth happens when we finally commit to mastery. Not a commitment to a goal, but to a purpose. That's when we stop doing *our* best and start doing *what's* best.

We are often doing the best we can, to achieve the best thing, when we should be doing the best thing, to achieve the best we can. Committing to mastery, to growth, is a consistent pursuit of improvement in all that you do. There's that word again, consistent. Pushing yourself to achieve more, physically, intellectually, and spiritually in an ongoing commitment. Not to amass an amount of wealth or possessions, but deep personal growth. Become a better leader, a better person, have empathy, compassion, and generosity. What you get, will never make you happy, but who you become in the process, certainly can.

It is up to us to grow in the process, to better ourselves beyond the goal, beyond the achievement, to something bigger.

We need to grow in order to contribute to something more substantial than ourselves. Giving to something outside of our own benefit, to a purpose bigger than just personal gain. It's real progress, with real purpose. It's the result of gratitude. The real expression of gratitude is real generosity. Doing something for someone else and expecting nothing in return. Absolutely nothing. Not even recognition. It's not about your own success; it's not even about you at all. It's about others. It's about understanding grace, feeling real gratitude for it, and wanting to do nothing else, but pour those same blessings out onto others. The experience of real gratitude will cause a person to want to give, not to receive. It's a completely selfless understanding. The secret to living is giving.

○　　○　　○

Giving – An outward expression of an inward emotion. Real purpose is learning to understand the spiritual aspect of contributing to something other than your own needs. It's literally referred to as the *spirit* of giving. I waited till now to discuss the aspect of human needs because I wanted you to build your previous written goals from the heart, from the soul. If you go back and look at those goals, those defined purposes you laid out for yourself, I'm willing to bet that you established a purpose that is larger than yourself. You'll see that with just a little direction, you wrote a purpose that was about providing, giving, or enriching others. Purposes that were to lead and provide for your family. Goals that would have a positive impression on those closest to you. Aspirations that were passionate about making an impact in others' lives. Those things will provide certainty, love and connection, significance, and contribution. Those goals that will meet certain human needs, give you the ability to grow as a person, and allow you the privilege of giving back to others that will absolutely change your life.

Those who are happiest, are those who do the most for others.

— Booker T. Washington

The secret to living really is giving. I truly believe that, and the best part is that you can start right now. Don't mislead yourself into thinking that when you finally receive, you will give. The person who wouldn't give a dime from a dollar, won't give thousands from a million. You don't need money to contribute to others; you just need you. You can give time, energy, and effort. Simon Sinek, a visionary thinker of our time, has a great example of this, in his description of how people feel and react to hearing about the donation of money versus the donation of time. He describes telling someone, you gave 20 dollars to a homeless person, and you might get a mild "oh good for you." However, tell someone you gave up your Saturday to paint a school, and you get an amazingly different response. Time and energy are non-redeemable commodities. They are far more valuable than any amount of money and carry a level of gratitude within them.

The influence of giving comes from the hormone oxytocin. A neuropeptide in the brain that's released with different forms of human interaction. It's commonly associated with physical touch, sexual pleasure, and social bonding, but it's far more complex than that. What you should take from it, is its feel-good capacity in terms of giving. Oxytocin is released when you act out of generosity. Real generosity, selfless giving of time and energy, not just money. Even in those simple acts of kindness, when no one else is looking. You can make an impact, and inspire people simultaneously. You can grow, as well as contribute to something beyond yourself. This is possible because every time you do something out of generosity you get that little bump of oxytocin, which makes you feel all warm and fuzzy inside. The best part is, so does the person that you're generous to. They too, get a little bump of oxytocin. You make impacts as you inspire.

You become a positive vehicle for someone else to meet their human needs. You become a blessing to others. When you encompass the spirit of giving, when you attempt to add value to others' lives, you can empower other people. By doing so, you will empower yourself. Be a vessel of what you want to see in the world. Be the outward expression of what's really inside you. Hold the door for people, say thank you when someone does something kind, smile and make eye contact with a stranger, all these *little* things change the course of a day. They change the course of a life.

Act not on your own intentions. When your purest intent is larger than yourself, it's accompanied by a profound insight. Regardless of how you may view grace or your own version of it, I urge you to acknowledge it and truly be grateful for receiving it. Express the full extent of your gratitude through giving and supporting those around you. The grace that you have received, those blessings, you can't help but want to sow that into someone else's life. The more you realize that you have received the gift of life, the more your life will be a gift to others

Rejoice in the Lord always; again I will say, rejoice. Let your reasonableness be known to everyone. The Lord is at hand; do not be anxious about anything, but in everything by prayer and supplication with thanksgiving let your requests be made known to God. And the Peace of God, which surpasses all understanding, will guard your hearts and your minds in Christ Jesus.

— Philippians 4:4-7

With an understanding of God's grace, you can live your life purposely for him. I have rewritten the daily morning ritual to describe to you the spiritual focus of gratitude, as a believer.

A MORNING RITUAL FOR THE BELIEVER

You're going to start the first three minutes with a breathing exercise that will center you and create focus. Place yourself in a calm, quiet setting free of distractions, and close your eyes. You can be seated or standing in this exercise; I personally prefer to sit. You're going to start with your arms held high above your head, hands open wide as you breathe in, and then pull them down, closing your hands as you forcefully exhale through your nose. Reach open hands back towards the sky as you breathe in, and then rapidly bring them back down as you forcefully exhale through your nose again. Continue this process for about 30 repetitions (30 seconds), and then stop. Place your hands on your lap, or at your sides with your palms up, keep your eyes closed and just relax. Relax, feel your body, feel the creation the Lord has made in you. God breathed the breath of life into you. You are but breath, an unending promise. With every breath, you let in God. Breathe. Return hands back up to the sky and start your breathing again for a total of three sets, about three minutes.

Continue to relax after your last set of breathing. Bring your hands to your chest and place them over your heart. Feel your heart, I mean truly feel it. Breathe it in. Give thanks to the Lord for your beating heart, for you know you don't deserve the life he has given you. Let everything that has breath, praise the Lord – Jesus, calling out with a loud voice, said "Father, into your hands I commit my spirit!" And having said this he breathed his last... You then breathed your first. Go to the Lord in prayer, giving thanks for his grace and mercy, that he has given you salvation. Spend as much *time as needed here, and just be grateful. Be grateful that you have a God, so loving, that he has given you mercy. Rejoice in your salvation and give thanks.*

Then I want you to find a couple of things or moments you can truly feel gratitude for. Spend another minute or two in prayer, really connecting with God and each one. Ask the Lord to continue to fill your heart with the Holy Spirit, worship him with gratitude for your salvation, your life, for family, friends, things you have been blessed with, and simply just the feeling of the sun on your face.

Then, in the last step, focus on three outcomes or results that you are really committed to. See yourself accomplishing them for the glory of God. Step into those moments with a full heart. Visualize the things you want to achieve, and picture yourself with each one completed. Let the full emotion of those achievements set in. Envision the impact those accomplishments have on those around you. Feel the gratitude in them. Be thankful for those moments and those blessings. Then go to God for his guidance. Ask the Lord to use you. Go to him in prayer, surrender to his will, and listen to his word. Pray for the wisdom and the resources, to help you accomplish these things, with the understanding that Jesus may not have the same plan for your life as you. See those things you want to achieve with certainty, but know the Lord and your salvation is the only thing truly certain in this world. I see it as an unfaltering approach to the outcomes I feel committed to: first God, then others, then me.

CHAPTER 7

MODEL THE MARINES

Never above you, never below you, always beside you.

— Walter Winchell

How does the Marine Corps take a group of strangers from different areas, with different backgrounds, and make them all initiate a massive change within themselves? How do they get them to care so much for one another, in such a short amount of time? So much so, that they are willing to lay down their life for the man next to them. The Marine Corps has created a fail-safe system of mindset, selflessness, and change. From the moment a young man steps onto the yellow footprints, the change begins. You no longer use words like I, me, and you. You immediately learn to speak in the third person, for you are no longer an individual. Where you came from doesn't matter, only where you're going. How you did things before is no longer relevant, only how you do them going forward. Whatever your prior beliefs were, are now meaningless. The story you're building now is all that matters. Whomever you thought you were going in, is now gone.

When a young man shows up to Marine Corps boot camp, no matter who he is, I can assure you he will experience fear, uncertainty, and most likely a small amount of regret for ever signing up. Most of us are teenagers, or in our early twenties. I personally, was only 17 years old when I stepped on that island. I can assure you that I had no idea what I was doing and was sure I didn't belong there. There's a small transition period that happens for all of us. The standard adaptation to training is usually a couple of weeks, trying to prove yourself as an individual, that you belong, that you can make it. However, training is generally devised for you to fail if you go at it alone. Simple daily tasks require a cohesive effort from everyone involved. Slowly you will see young men come together, put any differences aside, and work together as a single unit. Those who don't will be alienated by the rest.

Marine Corps boot camp, at Parris Island, is probably one of the most iconic military basic trainings in the world. It's the longest duration within the armed forces and widely respected for its severe levels of order and discipline. Every moment is filled with intense, purpose-driven action. Every day is timed out to the minute. Training has specific intent. Words like integrity, valor, fortitude, and loyalty are common. Their ethos is built on a foundation of values – *Honor, Courage, and Commitment.*

The end result, a man who can now refer to himself in the first person again, who's unrecognizable from the boy he was just three months prior. He may have been a criminal on the streets, a drop-out, a racist, a star athlete, or just an introverted bookworm. No matter who he was going in, the man that comes out on the other side is fearless, disciplined, and holds himself to a higher standard. He is considered a warrior, a leader amongst men, a United States Marine.

O   O   O

The Marines don't use some secret military mind manipulation. They focus on simple behaviors, and the process of how we as humans work and interact. Honestly, it's what we should model our personal lives after. It's a blueprint for life, and at the core of what I have actually laid out for you in this book. Yes, when you go step by step through the processes of everything we've discussed, it is nothing more than a boot camp for life. Boot camp is what changes a young man, and the processes here can be what changes you. The change is in an instant, but the transformation is a lifetime. The Marine Corps has taught me so much about life, through leadership, and responsibility. Beyond the process of everything we've discussed thus far, I'd like to share with you a set of guiding principles. Things I've picked up over my years spent in and around the Marine Corps. Beliefs to live by and values to incorporate into your daily life.

I've often heard the phrase "Noah didn't build the ark in a day." They would be correct, but many seem to fail to remember that Noah didn't build the ark when it was raining either. He built it for years and years, waiting for when the flood would come. He was in a constant pursuit of building on something greater than himself. Unlike Noah, we often tend to wait until we're forced to take action on something. We tend to be mostly reactive instead of proactive, only seeking to learn something once its presented itself. Learning to change a tire while on the side of the road staring at one, isn't the ideal time. We procrastinate, we make excuses, and we list every reason possible as to why it would probably be better to wait just one more day – *I'll do it tomorrow*. We usually think we will act on something when we're in a better position, at a better time. The issue is that most problems tend to worsen with time, and tomorrow will only bring its own set of new problems, regardless of your position.

Time – Our biggest and most valuable commodity. We cannot replace it, we cannot buy more of it, and we all get the same exact amount of it. No matter your race, gender, or creed, we all have the same exact amount. There are 24 hours in each and every day, no more, no less. What you do with it, is completely up to you. Time is something we take very seriously in the military. Time on target, time on station, time of attack, are all things that can influence a mission's success or failures.

Time and punctuality are not taken lightly because being a few minutes late can cost lives. Time was so vital in the Marines that it was almost counterproductive at times. An order would come down from the command level about an event taking place at 1500. That information would be passed on by descending levels of authority, each making sure there men were there 15 minutes early. Once this information was passed down through the ranks, you would have Marines standing around for an event, 3 hours early. Even in those rare but ridiculous extremes, I would rather be an hour early than a minute late. Being prompt is a direct reflection of your personal reliability. It is a direct testimony to your trustworthiness. **Trust may be built over time, but only if you can show up to specific ones.** There are a million quotes out there about showing up. They all seem to have their own version of how to say, just show up. I agree, just do it on time.

Don't show up to prove. Show up to improve.

— Simon Sinek

Right now – Two big factors come to mind when I think of time: right now, and then. Right now, is the time you need to take action. Right now, is the very moment we should do something, yet so many times we don't. It's when someone says they're fed up with their job, tired of living a certain way, or done with a relationship, and yet they go right back to it the next day. It's when we have a vision or a dream that we don't pursue because it just isn't the right time. Right now, is always the right time, because there is no such thing as the perfect moment. So, stop waiting for it. There may be a time that is better than the other, but you will have lost one important thing while waiting for it. Time.

We say in combat that a bad decision made now is better than a great decision made later. It's a very true statement because doing nothing will get you killed a lot faster than doing something. That is a metaphor for life. Sitting around waiting for the perfect time to come along, can kill. It can kill your ambition, kill your aspirations, and slowly let your dreams begin to fade away. All too often, when you do something that may not be perfect, or at the perfect time, but with good intention and with everything you've got, it ends up turning out to be pretty damn close. Right now, is when you need to start. Right now, is when you make changes and right now is when you seek fulfillment. Right now.

Then – If you go to the gym today and workout like a madman, when you come home and look in the mirror, you will see absolutely nothing. Not one single physical change will have happened, but we all tend to look to see if it did. When you come back from the gym the next day, you still won't see a thing. You may start to feel some changes, but nothing you can see. Maybe in a couple of weeks you will see something, some sort of visual validation to what you're doing, but very little. You cannot get into great physical shape over the weekend. Just as you cannot build a successful business in an afternoon. Nor can you build a loving relationship over dinner. These things take time. They take effort and they take consistency. No one big thing will lead to any one of these things either. No single meeting will catapult your business to success and no one exercise will give you rock hard abs. It is the little things done right, done consistently, over and over again.

We live in a world of instant gratification, where just about everything we want is on demand. That is not how progress, relationships, or change really works. Most of us overestimate what we can do in a year, and drastically underestimate what we can do in a decade. We limit ourselves to the short-term and fail to envision anything beyond it. We abandon good ideas, even when things are actually working because we didn't see the immediate results we anticipated. Expectations can ruin us, especially when they are time sensitive. Rome was not built in a day. You may not see any significant changes right now, but if you do the right things, the little things consistently, you will. Not now, but then.

Details – Marines understand that it's the little things that will provide you the most success in combat. It's the attention to detail. The small elements you'll end up overlooking if you focus only on the end state. It's the reason for gear inspections and the purpose of tedious combat rehearsals. It's the intentions behind extensive planning, thorough reconnaissance, and specified orders. Not only in combat, but in our way of life. It's why Marines are so meticulous with their uniforms, structured in their day to day operations, and systematic in every last detail. The little things done well and done consistently will lead to the bigger things being accomplished. When you set your goals, and look at fulfilling your purpose, attack the details. List, execute, and accomplish the small tasks, and the larger ones will get completed along the way.

In a commencement speech at the University of Texas, Admiral William H. McRaven, commander of U.S. Special Operations Command, said it best, "If you make your bed every morning you will have accomplished the first task of the day." His speech goes on with, "It will give you a small sense of pride, and it will encourage you to do another task and another and another. By the end of the day, that one task completed will have turned into many tasks completed. Making your bed will also reinforce the fact that little things in life matter. If you can't do the little things right, you will never do the big things right." It's a great tactic and poses a very simple question. How do you expect to make change if you can't even make your bed? Be thorough in all that you do. God is in the details.

Standards – The Marines pride themselves in claiming to be the best of the armed forces. It's common banter to say that you only joined the Marine Corps so that you could talk trash to the other services. This amusing anecdote is based on one simple thing, standards. Holding ourselves to a higher standard is engrained in each of us at a cultural level. As a platoon sergeant, I would task a Marine with making a quick and simple roster.

If he brought me a torn scratch piece of paper, something hastily written, or even if it were just in blue ink, I would simply send him away. Of course, the list itself was most likely sufficient for its use, but it was the principle I wanted to instill in him. The idea of demanding the highest level of performance, even in the small and mundane.

Taking pride of ownership in your work and holding yourself to a higher standard will set you apart. Complete tasks to the very best of your ability, especially the small details, and accept nothing less. All too often, I hear people complaining about areas of their lives that they just aren't pleased with, like jobs, finances, or relationships. Yet, they don't seem to change their standards, they just accept them. They don't raise the bar so to speak. If you find yourself unhappy with your results, you most likely need to raise your standards. Example: If you're unhappy with your current position and looking to land a promotion at work, you need to hold yourself to that standard now. Not when you get the job, but now. You need to be at the appropriate level of education and understanding now. You need to be knowledgeable on the policies and expectations associated with that position now. You even need to look the part. Yes, look like you already have the position. Be a professional. Raise your standards, and hold yourself to them.

Position – When defending yourself in battle, you always want to harden your position. Meaning, you want to make every effort to ensure its the most defendable it can be. You build up barriers and add sandbags to posts. You walk terrain looking for things that may pose possible threats, disseminate ammunition and supplies, and safeguard sensitive materials. All these things apply, whether you're going to be there for five days, or five months. It's a never-ending process, an ongoing task that is never complete. Marines will continually seek to improve their positions and that's the exact same approach you and I should take every single day. To seek improvements in where you are as a person, should be a constant and ongoing task. This is the mindset to continually grow as an individual.

You must protect your heart and mind, by persistently improving your position. We say that complacency kills, because it does, literally and figuratively. It just depends on the battlefield.

Remember, when we stop growing, we start dying. That is why becoming complacent can be deadly. Don't confuse complacent with content. They are similar but very different. Being content with your life is perfectly ok, in fact, it's great. One can be completely satisfied with their finances, with their business, also pleased with their family and friends. You can have all that, be perfectly content, and still continue to grow. Being complacent though is different, it can sneak up on you, and it's dangerous. When complacency takes a hold, the mundane becomes the center of life, routine is more robotic than structured, and life becomes a revolving door of days. The only differentiating factor between the two is simple growth.

In tactical training, I often refer to the mindset of the complacent with that of cattle. Head down, slowly meandering through life, just eating the grass at their feet. They are completely oblivious to the world around them, and in combat that can be very dangerous. Complacency is a state that you reach when you no longer seek to improve your position. It's when growth is no longer a priority. The drive to be better than you were ceases and you become transfixed in your current existence. This is not about money, success, or status. You don't need to aspire to any of these things to grow intellectually, physically, or spiritually. Every exercise completed, every book read, and every moment of gratitude taken is time spent improving your position. Never stop seeking to improve your position. Leave things better than you found them, including yourself.

The master is forever the student.

— Robert Kiyosaki

Knowledge – A term thrown around the Marine Corps, more like it's a tangible item than a sense of understanding. We brand books with it as the title. Binders full of history, information, tactics, and procedures, all notoriously labeled as a book of knowledge. If you're unsure about a particular technique or piece of equipment, and you're going to be told to go and find some knowledge on that subject real fast. It's a quest to know, a journey to understanding. To know your job as well as the man above you and the man beside you. To understand your history as well as the world today. It is the principle of committing to mastery and the Marine Corps embodies it.

So, what is mastery? Is it a level of attainment, or is it a level of thinking? To commit to mastery, you're committing yourself to continually pursue an education. Not formal education in the sense of terms, but to simply educate yourself. That very well may be through an institution of higher learning, but it isn't necessary. It's a belief system. It's a journey back to the beginning of the book and understanding the seeds you plant in your garden. Your mind will continue to grow with you or without you. It is up to you to determine what grows in it. Are you feeding your mind sound doctrine? Are you stimulating your intellectual growth or are you just feeding it the daily nonsense that presents itself?

I told you about the exercise habits of some of the most successful people in the world. When you take a look at some of the top business leaders in our world you will see that as a common trend in most of them. However, the common trend in nearly all of them is of a different exercise. They all exercise their minds. Nearly every successful person I have met, studied, or read about, has the same characteristic when it comes to personal growth. They all read, and read excessively. Bill Gates states he reads one book a week. Mark Cuban estimates he reads about three hours per day. Warren Buffet and David Rubenstein read hours of newspapers and financial documents. Elon Musk, Mark Zuckerberg, Oprah Winfrey, are all avid daily readers. It's estimated that the average CEO reads nearly 50 books per year. Each choosing to read education over entertainment. They read for self-improvement and to further increase their knowledge.

Successful people don't read novels for entertainment, or tabloids, or lifestyle magazines. They read to better themselves. Reading is the gateway to learning and continuing to grow. There are many benefits of incorporating reading into your daily habits. Beyond increasing vocabulary and writing skills, increased reading leads to an increased ability to focus. It provides a form of stress relief, an ability to tune out the world and recharge your mind. Reading has been shown to increase memory and analytical thinking. By reading different works of literature, a reader can gain new perspectives, be more reflective, and learn to evaluate matters from all angles. Readers have a proactive mind, more capable of handling issues as they arise, and not waiting to educate themselves after the fact. Your mind, your garden, is always seeking to grow. Reading is the seed and the key to personal growth.

Ranger File – When patrolling through an area known to be laden with improvised explosive devices, or IEDs, it's common practice to follow the man in front of you. In most cases, this goes against all tactics associated with fire and maneuver but is necessary due to the IED threat. This type of formation, where one man follows directly behind another, is referred to as a ranger file. Instead of each man trying to detect possible IEDs and navigate through the streets, only one man does, leading from the front, and everyone else follows in trace. To avoid a grave mistake, each man walks by placing his foot in the boot print of the man in front of him. He literally follows in his footsteps. Sometimes in life, the path to success would be much shorter, if we would just follow the footsteps of those who have gone before us.

Look to the people who have accomplished the same goals you've set for yourself. Find those who have already forged the way ahead, and mimic their ideas and strategies. The people who are successful in their particular field are obviously doing something right. Analyze those things and apply them to your life. A mentor can be an instrumental part of your success. Find one, study them, read about them, learn from their successes, and their failures. Arnold Schwarzenegger said, "the self-made man is a myth." No one is self-made and anyone who claims to be is lying to you and themselves. Even the most successful people, who rose from nothing, had help getting there. If not directly, then most certainly indirectly. There will be people who will help you along the way, and at the very least, inspire you. So, seek guidance, ask for advice, and follow the people who have led the way. Replicate the qualities of those you wish to emulate and form the best decisions and strategies that you can for yourself. Regardless of where or who you draw your inspiration from, your actions will be all your own.

Accountability – After every combat operation, Marines will conduct a debrief to discuss the evolution that just took place. We will go from beginning to end, discussing each person's involvement and responsibilities, and what transpired from different vantage points. Giving us the ability to identify key elements that led to our possible successes or failures. We would begin any tactical debrief by collectively examining the initial assessment of our situation. That may have been from a radio transmission that came in, an order that was given, or a situation we encountered first hand. What information did we have and what beliefs did we derive from it? Then we would examine how accurate that information was from reality and if or how that should have changed our beliefs. Only then can the team take the appropriate actions to improve or continue our operational success. It's a growth mindset.

This assessment can only be done by having each individual Marine give his account of the operation. What one man may have seen, or thought he saw, could be completely different from the man who experienced it directly, and vice versa. Multiple vantage points provide the most information in order to come to the most accurate conclusion of the events that took place. This is imperative in order to mitigate issues, adapt to surroundings, and increase their overall success. They can then leave each debrief with vital takeaways. As you continue to grow in life, grow in knowledge, take on new business ventures, or new relationships, you need to conduct your own personal debriefs as well. Always find the takeaways from every situation, good or bad.

Those takeaways are for you, for your own self-assessment, and your own personal growth. They are an honest look at what actions need to be taken to achieve the desired outcome. Not a single outside element ever resulted in a combat mission's failure, not one. That doesn't mean that outside elements never affected a mission, it means they were never the cause of the outcome. Bad weather just meant you needed to plan and train for bad weather. Bad maps meant you needed to find another way. Bad intelligence and outdated satellite imagery meant things might be different than what you initially expected. Get over it, and carry on. Circumstances will not dictate the outcomes of the United States Marines and they shouldn't for you either. Be accountable for you. I heard Gary Vaynerchuk once say at a seminar, "I critique everything I do. Everything is my fault. Period, end of story." He goes on to say, "If somebody hits me with a car tomorrow, I'm like, I shouldn't have left the house that early." **Complete accountability**.

Now, obviously Gary's latter point is a bit excessive, but it just goes to show you the level of personal responsibility, some of the most successful people carry. He critiques everything he does. He conducts a personal debrief and doesn't succumb to the notion of outside factors dictating his results. He holds himself personally liable for every action, even to the point that getting hit by a car would be considered his fault. This may be a bit of an exaggeration, but the point remains the same. He then said in that same seminar, "You get into that mindset, and I promise you things change." I can make you that same promise. **Create the appropriate mindset, and things will change.**

O   O   O

The Marine Corps has obviously left a huge impact on my life and I carry many of their principles with me to this day. I challenge you to do the same. To live by these principles in your daily actions and strive to be the best version of yourself that you can. Understand that time is all we have. Value it, because you have a limited supply. So, spend it wisely. Respect the time of others and be punctual. Take action now, right now. There is no better time than the present. Put the time in and be consistent in your actions. Consistency will be the biggest influencer of change and can move mountains over time. Never limit yourself to an unrealistic timeframe. **Time – Respect it, Value it, Use it.**

Never overlook the details. The little things will usually make the biggest difference. This is only done when you hold yourself, and your work, to a higher standard. Take pride in ownership of everything you do. Complete every task to the very best of your ability, even when it's just making the bed. Do this and you will begin to see the residual effects of your behaviors. You will begin to consistently and continually improve your position. Always seek to leave things better than you found them. Pursue daily improvement in every aspect of your life. Seek knowledge. Forever be the student. Give your garden everything it needs to flourish. Commit to mastery! Don't neglect to conduct a debrief and evaluate your situation from every angle. Do it early, do it often, and do it with a growth mindset. Be 100% accountable for your actions and your outcome. In the words of William Ernest Henley, you are the master of your fate, the captain of your soul.

CHAPTER 8
MASTERING MINDSET

What the mind of man can conceive and believe, it can achieve.

— Napoleon Hill

The real power of mindset is only recently being discovered and may quite possibly be limitless in its effects. The power of the mind is truly unmeasurable and something we are just beginning to learn how to understand. I'm not talking about the popular myth of using only 10% of our brains, or any other ridiculous correlation between intelligence and brain usage. All of us, use all of our brain, all the time. It's the capacity and the manner in which we use it that holds our greatest potential. That conceivable quality roots itself in our mindset. The beliefs we live by, the truths we have come to understand, and the certainties of our minds.

Mindset has been shown, through multiple studies, to have astounding impacts on our emotions, our perceptions, and even change our biology. Think about that for a second. Your mind has the ability to alter your physiology, just by the way you think. The implication of your thoughts, of your beliefs, are that powerful. Mindset has the ability to change your life all its own. A single thought can change my physical nature? You may think, I'm completely out of my mind, and you'd be right. I am out of my mind, and subsequently in complete control of it now

So many of us are trapped in our own minds and limited by our belief systems, which usually aren't even accurate. I've said to you throughout this book, that your thoughts can, and will, become your reality. Mindset is everything. Whatever your perceived notions are, of any given thing, the likelihood in the actuality of that outcome increases exceptionally.

There are two main products of a misguided mind, an altered reality, and damaged expectations. Either can bring about real issues with your health, your state, and your overall quality of life, but expectations can kill. They can kill a relationship, sack your motivation, and ruin just about any experience. There will be certain times in our relationships; we feel hurt or angered by something someone else has done. All too often, that feeling is derived from what wasn't done, over what was. We are hurt when someone didn't respond or act in the manner in which we envisioned. It didn't meet our expectations. Many times, that person didn't really do anything to hurt or anger us, but it was our own mindset that made it feel so. Our own expectations can be the cause of our own suffering. I'm not implying that you limit your expectations. I'm merely stating to manage them with the appropriate mindset. This is done in three parts, **preparation, expectation, and optimism.**

O   O   O

The effects of the mind have been shown through countless studies that demonstrate how the appropriate mindset can alter our reality and vice versa. In clinical research, this has been commonly displayed with the placebo effect. The basic premise is that a particular placebo, like a sugar pill, with no known medical effects, is administered, yet still results in response to treatment. Our minds being so powerful that our anticipated response of treatment actually produces a positive benefit from nothing. This all well and true, but nothing really groundbreaking. The understanding of the placebo effect has been around for quite some time. The real kicker is the mind's effect in the opposite manner as well. That the lack of expectation can also have an effect on actual treatment.

If a placebo has an effect, is it any less real than the real thing?

— Nathaniel LeTonnerre

A study was done with two groups of post-operative patients and their pain management treatment. One group received scheduled pain medication, administered bedside by a doctor. While the other group received identical medication and dosages but was administered intravenously through an automated pump. Both groups were given the exact same medication, same dose, same amount, and administered at the same times. Yet the group that was aware of the pain management treatment reported a far greater decrease in pain symptoms than the group that had no idea they were receiving it. They went through the same operation, received the same treatment, and were given the same pain medication, yet the pain they experienced was completely different. Mindset changes everything. Now, the researchers went on to test this theory against anxiety, Parkinson's, and hypertension. The results were identical. When patients knew of the treatment being received the benefits of medication were clearly seen in results. However, when they were not aware of any treatment, the results were minimal, if not non-existent.

Our mind's ability to perceive a level of treatment that's happening, when there isn't any real treatment being received is one thing, but the mind's ability to make actual treatment ineffective opens up a whole other realm. It puts the understanding of the placebo effect on its head. Let me give you another example of this. Another study was done in regard to exercise, with a group of hotel housekeepers. They were all asked if they exercised, with more than two-thirds responding, "no." These are women, who are on their

121

feet all day long, working hard, using a number of muscles, and burning a large number of calories, yet none of them viewed their work as exercise. All the women were measured and tested in multiple facets and then divided into two groups. One group was given a presentation on the benefits of exercise and how their work qualified as such, so they should expect the same results as they would from exercise. The other group was given no guidance as the control. With no other factors added to their lifestyle, the first group saw a reduction in weight, body fat, and blood pressure, while even reporting that they found their jobs more satisfying.

The study references that our mindset can literally alter our physiology. The understanding that merely the perception of exercise, can actually cause the physical effects associated with it. This opens the question to all things being a placebo. Are we only benefitting from exercise because we perceive it to be so? Now, this may be a stretch, but it shows the impact our minds can have on the human body. I'll go one further on the power of mindset in clinical research. Another study was done on a group of volunteers, on the effects and perceptions of hunger. A test group was given two different milkshakes at two different times, while they were simultaneously being tested for ghrelin. Ghrelin is a peptide that increases to signal hunger, and let us know it's time to eat. The test subjects were given one shake and the information on it, a low calorie, fat-free shake (*140 calories*). Ghrelin levels dropped a minimal amount, as expected with a low-calorie shake. The same group was brought back at a later time to test the second shake, a high calorie, high fat, high sugar shake (*620 calories*). As expected, ghrelin levels dropped significantly. The catch is that at both times the test subjects were given the exact same milkshake both times (*380 calories*), yet the body reacted completely different to the same shake.

That's how much of an impact our mindset can have on our bodies. Our thoughts can impact us in ways you probably didn't even think were possible. Take for instance, thinking about food. We all have heard someone say, if not you yourself, that just looking at certain foods will make them fat. Well, they might be right. That box of donuts in the office can be far worse than you might think. When you consume sugar, your body releases insulin to utilize that sugar for energy, while regulating blood sugar levels, and storing any that's unused. Did you know, that when you think you're about to eat something sweet, your body begins to produce insulin in preparation? It's called the cephalic phase insulin release (CPIR). Just by seeing or smelling food, your body begins to react to your mind's own perceptions of it. If you are constantly thinking about sweet foods, or imagining all the things you miss while on a diet, you're doing a lot more harm than you think. When your insulin runs high, but there isn't any sugar being consumed, it resorts to its other job of storing it as fat. So, yeah. Looking at food can make you fat, or even just thinking about it.

O   O   O

I hope you' can see how particular conditions can have little to no effect on our outcome if our thoughts are not properly aligned. How we think, how we view things, how we manage our expectations in life, is the key to positive outcomes. Mindset is vital. All the education in the world is not going to prepare you for life, if you are not mentally prepared to live it. All the training in the world is not going to prepare you for war if you are not mentally prepared for battle. Whether it be daily life or combat operations, the power lies in your state of mind.

Nothing is more crucial to conducting successful operations in combat than having the appropriate mindset. That mindset can only come from understanding how to condition yourself to handle certain expectations and perceptions. When a warrior steps on to the battlefield, he must make peace with his death and its certainty. He doesn't need to feel he will die or must die. He just needs to understand it, accept it, and reconcile its possibility. Once he has achieved that mental state, he can now make sound tactical decisions with a clear mind. He doesn't act out of fear or anger, rather logic and intelligence. He must come to terms with the violence he will encounter and bring himself to violent actions as well. He must understand that casualties are probable, and his decisions could possibly make the difference between the wounded and the dead. He must understand this, be prepared for it, and then operate with an unrelenting optimism, that it will never happen.

This is the exact mindset you must carry on the battlefield of life as well. Not in the terms of violence or casualties, but in preparation and optimism. Life will not always be perfect, that is quite apparent and nothing too profound, but the way we handle those imperfections are. Conditioning your mind to know that you will undoubtedly encounter adversity, face hardships, experience rejection, and most likely know certain failures, will be the key to real happiness. It may seem to be counterintuitive to prepare for failures in order to achieve successes but it really is essential. Just like the warrior, you must accept certain aspects of your life that are inevitable, prepare for them, and manage the expectations of those outcomes. Simultaneously, living your life with the optimism of those things never happening.

Our expectations can destroy us, or enlighten us. Operating on the battlefield with the expectation that everyone is going to die, will never work. Why go into battle, why leave the safety of a secured camp? You'll stay right there in the safety of going nowhere. On the other hand, leaving the base with the expectations that no one will ever get hurt will leave you shattered if and when that day comes. However, stepping off with an optimistic outlook of smooth success and safety, with the security of knowing that you're more than ready if it's not, is what will keep you going. That's the mindset that works for you, not against you. If you fear failure, if you expect hardship, then you will stay right where you're at, where it's safe. If you think you will always succeed all the time, you will be crushed when you finally fail. The key is to attack every goal, every task, and every day, with wild optimism, that is rooted in managed expectations.

On the battle field, the most intense and chaotic moments bring about the most heroic and courageous actions. Those actions are derived from a mental response associated with stress. How does one man thrive in the face of adversity, and another man cower? It's the mindset towards high-stress environments. Stress is culturally viewed as a risk to health, damaging to our psyche, and a hindrance to performance. If we really analyze stress though, we could find that it typically causes a positive reaction. For you to increase strength, you have to place your muscles under stress. For you to increase cognitive abilities, you have to introduce certain stressors to improve your rational intellect. Some of the most memorable and amazing sports plays, came in high-stress moments. The most selfless and intrepid acts of man, I have had the blessings to witness, came at the peak of a stressful environment.

Studies have shown the differences in stress, eustress (positive) versus distress, and the resulting factors of both. Some of the benefits of eustress are focused energy, improved performance, heightened awareness, and increased blood flow and oxygen. This is because the stress is perceived to be within our coping skills, and usually associated with some form of reward. For example, starting a new job, getting married, or taking the game-winning shot with just seconds remaining. These are all high-stress scenarios, but presumably manageable with a possibility of reward. With that understanding, what if we could associate all stress with a perceived reward and manageable outcome? We could encounter all stress with positivity, and then it would actually improve our health, cognitive function, and disposition. This is essentially adopting a growth mindset, outside of the learning environment, and introducing it to daily life. Every time you're presented with a potentially stressful situation, you need to analyze things for their reward, for the possible lessons and learning experience involved. Each and every time you encounter these situations, and you buckle down to persevere through them, the radius of your comfort zone increases. Your ability to cope with certain situations increases.

Through managed expectations and perceptions, you'll have the ability to view most stressful situations as being within your comfort zone. That increased coping ability reduces any anxiety that would have been associated with them. By adopting a growth mentality towards adversity, you'll be able to value the learning experience and see the increase in your resilience. You've seen the power of the mind and should be able to conclude that the appropriate mindset, regarding stress, can limit any adverse symptoms, if not eliminate them all together.

Your mindset can be the difference between winning and losing, or even living and dying. Every bit of information studied, and every minute spent training, means nothing if you haven't yet conditioned your mind. A fighter with all the talent and skill in the world will be crushed without the will or mindset to fight. Yet, the man with little, to no training, can triumph with an undying will to survive and the mindset to battle against all odds. Mindset is simply a prepared acceptance to potentials. A fighter knows he will get hit in the face, and so he prepares for it. That same fighter also trains to avoid it. Understanding probabilities and then adapting to mitigate or capitalize on them. That's all mindset really is. Many see this as fortitude or other aspects of someone's natural character, and many times it is, but it can be learned, it can be conditioned. You must condition your mind to the possibilities in your life. Prepare yourself mentally for daily living and to chase your biggest dreams. Be able to weather any storm, and you'll find yourself always in the sun.

CHAPTER 9
THE RIPPLE EFFECT

Drop a pebble in the water: just a splash, and it is gone;
But there's half-a-hundred ripples circling on and on and on...

— James W. Foley

Drop a stone into water and it will be gone in an instant, but its impact is far greater than the little splash it will make. A splash on the surface, but as the stone sinks deeper, the water begins to ripple farther and farther out. Even the smallest of pebbles will cause a ripple effect. Everything you have learned thus far has the same principle as the stone. Each action will cause a splash on the surface, some small, some large, but they will all descend much deeper. That's precisely the effect that occurs when you apply the principles in this book. You must start with you. The ability to improve your physicality is the first step in lasting change. That change, that splash, will have a ripple effect and overflow into every other area of your life. The discipline that is created in the process will be the discipline that drives you to your purpose. Purpose, that's where we initially started. I hope that by the end of this book you have a clear understanding of what that is for you, in all walks of life. I'm confident that if you were paying attention, you'll realize that this purpose should be bigger than just yourself.

The Bible is clear that God created man, and he created him for his glory. We were created for God's glory. Therefore, our sole purpose is to glorify God. That is where you will find your ultimate fulfillment. In everything you do, in every dream you pursue, do it for the glory of God. **Be selfless.** If you aren't a believer, at a minimum, recognize that you weren't put on this earth for your own pleasure. There is a purpose for your life that is greater than you. As you begin to fulfill that purpose, nothing will bring you greater joy in life, than to enrich someone else's. With your own personal goals, look to provide, before you strive to attain. More often than not, the latter will come as you pursue the former. Be honest in your pursuit though. You cannot lie to the only two people in your life that truly matter, God and yourself. You must be honest about your intentions, and sincere in your actions. **Be truthful.**

Understand that your mind is a beautiful garden, all your own. You have the ability to plant and cultivate whatever you want. Make sure you plant good seed and care for it daily, or the weeds will take over. This is so important to our growth, and to our state of mind. The different forms of media we take in will have a deep impact on our ideology. Choose what your mind is exposed to wisely. Let your moral compass guide you to things of a positive and decent nature. **Be intuitive.** We should want to seek knowledge before entertainment. Our culture is shifting, and we need to be wary of where it's headed. A society obsessed with pop culture, scripted reality, and using social media as its source of knowledge and entertainment, is disheartening. We live in a world full of information, and we should view it as a blessing. Full libraries in our homes, machines that can answer any question we may ask, and an endless source of information right in the palm of our hand. **Be grateful.** Utilize every bit of it to be the forever student. Commit yourself to mastery, and seek the knowledge that will improve your life. Read every single day. Read to be informed. Read for the experience. Change the status of our culture, and strive to be an intellectual, over being someone famous. Education should be a never-ending pursuit. **Be enlightened.** You must be mindful of the educational tools and resources you use. We have to manage what we let in, filter the media that is forced upon us, and fill our minds with the things that support our purpose. Anything that doesn't fit that purpose must go.

Cleaning out the kitchen pantry was a literal metaphor for life. To get a handle on your nutrition, you needed to rid your kitchen from all the unhealthy items that plagued your health. It's what many of us need to do in our personal lives as well, in order to rid ourselves of the "junk food" holding us back. The cupboards of our minds and our lives tend to be filled with the garbage we have picked up along the way. No different than your kitchen is your own personal pantry. Rid yourself of anyone and anything that doesn't align with the person you are, the goals you have, and how you see yourself. Prepare yourself for the naysayers, for the opposition from friends and family, and the opinionated responses you will receive along the way. They mean nothing to your journey and that's exactly how you should value them. Your dreams far outweigh anyone's opinions. **Be ambitious.**

Wild ambition is not new to you, nor is envisioning your dreams. Look at children, or remember yourself as an adolescent. Look back at your room, most likely filled with posters, pictures, and items that inspired you. Whether you wanted to be a star athlete or an astronaut, I bet you had things all over your room that inspired you to do so. Why would that change with adulthood? Somewhere along the line, we tend to lose our innate inspiration and our views begin to change. For some reason, hanging inspirational signs and photos on the wall and dreaming of wild accomplishments just seems childish. It's sad really, that we would allow our dreams to become a laughable memory of our youth. In some sort of twisted irony, the posters of your childhood dreams are reduced to an arbitrary nature scene that says – TEAMWORK, hanging in a corporate office. I've never encountered a single person that was truly inspired by an office meme. Although, I have met many people who were inspired by their childhood ones. **Be inspired.** Fill your life with things that motivate you, drive you, and remind you every day of what it is you truly want. Live your life with childlike ambition. Prime yourself for explosive change. Build that daily priming system that motivates action. Create the daily triggers that will drive you towards success, and pursue life with a vigor.

Consistency is the key to so many different aspects of life. To create lasting change, you must be consistent. To establish a solid relationship, you must be consistent. To build daily habits, you must be consistent. A daily routine provides focus, and energy flows where focus goes. Anything you pursue in life will only come from a determined and consistent effort. Routine builds discipline, the discipline to persevere, to endure hardship, and overcome challenges. It's what will set you apart from the rest of the field. There may be others more talented, someone else may be more gifted, but there is no reason for anyone to ever outwork you. **Be disciplined.** When opportunity presents itself, know that you are ready, and be confident in your abilities. Remember that the real law of attraction is simply the moment when optimistic preparation meets opportunity. **Be prepared.**

In everything you do, in all that you aspire to be and accomplish, always maintain a level of humility and appreciation for all that you have. Gratitude is vital to your happiness. It's the one single thing that can provide the most benefit to your life. Health, emotional, social, personal, all benefit from gratitude. It will be the center of your deepest sense of fulfillment and should be the focus of your daily living. **Be thankful.** Take in every day, see the world around you, breathe it in, and be grateful for the opportunity to live in it just one more day.

Every day you have choices, you have decisions that will shape who you are, and what you become. These are your decisions, and yours alone. You are responsible for your own life. We are defined by our decisions, not by our circumstances.

Be decisive. Circumstances will only affect you as much as you allow them to. Many people will say you can't control your surroundings, but I hope you can see by now, that you can. You may not have direct control of outside elements, nor should you try to, but you actually do have control of so much more. You have control of the environment you put yourself into. You have control of your disposition towards your surroundings. You have control of the people you associate with, the ones you let into your personal life, and those who you choose to spend your time with. You have control of what you put into your body. Most importantly you have the power over your own mindset. How you live your life and the state you choose to live it in, is the ultimate control. That state of mind will affect everything in, and around your life. So yes, you do have control of your surroundings. You have control of your state.

Take each step we discussed and hold yourself accountable for your thoughts and actions. Prepare for life, as you would for combat. Commit to mastery. Take the appropriate steps that need to be taken in order to reach your goals. Remove the distractions, raise your standards, prepare yourself, and build those daily habits. Do these things consistently and you will see them overflow into every facet of your life, and the ripple effect that will take place. As you begin to close this chapter and start a new one in your own story, I challenge you to do just one thing. At the very least, live your life beautifully. The world out there is beautiful if you're looking in the right places. There are so many beautiful people in this world, including yourself. Fill your life with that beauty. Create that mindset, a mindset for life, a beautiful life. Live each day in a beautiful state. Be beautiful, be kind, be honest, be generous, be fruitful, be compassionate, be positive, be a leader, be a warrior...

BE RELENTLESS.

WRITING EXERCISES

I've given you an area to work on the specific writing exercises we discuss in the early chapters, as well as a place for you to write down the things you may find of value along the way.

_____

_____

_____

_____

_____

_____

NOTES

NOTES

NOTES

NOTES

A MESSAGE TO THE WARRIOR

We all left who we originally were at some point to head off to a place far from home, to do a job with a purpose we thought was far greater than ourselves. It's in the selfless nature of a warrior to do this willingly and with great pride. Regardless of the feelings why you went, we all know the reason why you stayed to fight. The same reason any of us would do it all over again. The bonds we create during war know no bounds.

Greater love has no one than this, that someone lay down his life for his friends.

— John 15:13

Many of us experienced things we may have never wanted to see. Many of us had to do things we never thought we would have to do. Most of us adapted in any way we deemed necessary to continue to operate at the highest levels. Many times, that meant writing a new story for ourselves. A story that may have stated that what we left behind at home was no longer there. Our fate would now be determined in battle. I know that was my story. I removed fear from the equation because I had fully accepted my fate, as I should. That mindset allowed me to operate with far greater efficiency. This kind of mentality is common amongst warriors. It's what many of us have done knowingly or not. The problem with this mindset is that its purpose ceased the moment we returned home. So many of us, so good at writing our story and shaping our mindset for battle, never rewrote the story on the trip home.

We end up back with our friends and families, sitting at home with the same mindset we had patrolling the battle field. We lack a sense of purpose and still have the story of our life in combat. We see our brothers struggle day in and day out wondering their purpose and confused by their existence. Maybe this is how you feel. If you do, you have to look at your story. Are you still operating under the same set of beliefs? Do you still have the same purpose? A warrior's purpose is war. Look at those basic human needs again. War will make you feel significant immediately. There is a certainty in your mission. Your purpose, your time there, those around you that you can depend on are all certain. Yet, war comes with all sorts of variety too. You feel the greatest sense of connection in the bonds you have with your brothers. Your purpose feels bigger than yourself, and you would willingly do anything for the man to your right or left. War can meet every human need at some of the highest levels you will ever experience.

Knowing that can help you understand the void you may be experiencing. You won't be able to fill it. You need to rewire your mind. You have to define a new purpose for your life, but more importantly you have to rewrite your story. You must change your mindset to operate at the most efficient levels for home now. You will always be a warrior but you have to find a new war. Pick a new battle and attack it head on. Those you can serve are in your community and your brothers are now your friends and family. Find your purpose. Rewrite your story. You may never face anything like you did in combat again, and that's okay. You served your time, you fought your battle, now it's time for a new one. **Change your Story – Change your Life.**

Semper Fi,

146

RESOURCES

Holy Bible: English Standard Version. (2001). Wheaton, IL: Crossway Bibles.

Allen, J. (1921). *As a Man Thinketh*. New York: H.M. Caldwell Co.

Karlin, M. (2015). *The Simplicity of Stillness Method: 3 Steps to Rewire Your Brain, and Access Your Highest Potential*. London: Watkins

Dweck, C. S. (2006). *Mindset: The New Psychology of Success*. New York: Random House.

Maltz, M. (1960). *Psycho-cybernetics*. New York: Pocket Books, Simon and Schuster.

Kissin, B. (1986). *Conscious and Unconscious Programs in the Brain. (Psychobiology of Human Behavior; v. 1)* New York: Plenum Med. Book Co.

Garcia-Rill, E. (2015). *Waking and the reticular activating system in health and disease*. Amsterdam: Elsevier.

Matthews, G. (2015). The Effectiveness of Four Coaching Techniques in Enhancing Goal Achievement: Writing Goals, Formulating Action Steps, Making a Commitment, and Accountability. In *Psychology Abstracts: Ninth Annual International Conference on Psychology* (p. 41). Athens, Greece: Athens Institute for Education and Research.

Locke, E. A., Shaw, K. N., Saari, L. M., & Latham, G. P. (1981). Goal setting and task performance: 1969–1980. *Psychological Bulletin, 90*(1), 125-152.

Steinberg, K. (2016). The Harris Poll #50 American Happiness Index.

RESOURCES

Tubbs, M. E. (1986). Goal setting: A meta-analytic examination of the empirical evidence. *Journal of Applied Psychology, 71*(3), 474-483

Dalton, A., & Spiller, S. (2012). Too Much of a Good Thing: The Benefits of Implementation Intentions Depend on the Number of Goals. *Journal of Consumer Research, 39*(3), 600-614.

Wing, R., Phelan, S. (2005). Long-term weight-loss maintenance. *The American Journal of Clinical Nutrition.* 2005 Jul;82(1):222S-225S.

Anderson, J., Konz, E., Frederich, R., Wood, C. (2001). Long-term weight-loss maintenance: a meta-analysis of US studies. *The American Journal of Clinical Nutrition.* 2001 Nov;74(5):579-84.

Montesi, L., El Ghoch, M., Brodosi, L., Calugi, S., Marchesini, G., & Dalle Grave, R. (2016). Long-term weight loss maintenance for obesity: a multidisciplinary approach. *Diabetes, Metabolic Syndrome and Obesity: Targets and Therapy, 9,* 37–46.

Ratey, J. & Loehr, J. (2011). The positive impact of physical activity on cognition during adulthood: a review of underlying mechanisms, evidence and recommendations. *Reviews in the Neurosciences, 22*(2), pp. 171-185.

Forwood, S. E., Ahern, A. L., Hollands, G. J., Ng, Y.-L., & Marteau, T. M. (2015). Priming healthy eating. You can't prime all the people all of the time. *Appetite, 89,* 93–102.

Friedman, R., Elliot, A. (2008). Exploring the influence of sports drink exposure on physical endurance. *Psychology of Sport and Exercise, 9*(6), 749-759.

Berger, J., Meredith, M., & Wheeler, S. C. (2008). Contextual priming: Where people vote affects how they vote. *Proceedings of the National Academy of Sciences of the United States of America, 105*(26), 8846–8849. http://doi.org/10.1073/pnas.0711988105

Bargh, J. A., Chen, M., & Burrows, L. (1996). Automaticity of social behavior: Direct effects of trait construct and stereotype activation on action. *Journal of Personality and Social Psychology, 71*(2), 230-244.

Doyen S, Klein O, Pichon C-L, Cleeremans A (2012) Behavioral Priming: It's All in the Mind, but Whose Mind? PLoS ONE7(1): e29081.

Benedetti, F., Pollo, A., Lopiano, L., Lanotte, M., Vighetti, S., & Rainero, I. (2003). Conscious Expectation and Unconscious Conditioning in Analgesic, Motor, and Hormonal Placebo/Nocebo Responses. *Journal of Neuroscience.*

Crum, A. J., Corbin, W. R., Brownell, K. D., & Salovey, P. (2011). Mind over milkshakes: Mindsets, not just nutrients, determine ghrelin response. *Health Psychology, 30*(4), 424-429.

Crum, A. J., & Langer, E. J. (2007). Mind-Set Matters. *Psychological Science, 18*(2), 165-171.

Crum, A. J., Salovey, P., & Achor, S. (2013). Rethinking stress: The role of mindsets in determining the stress response. *Journal of Personality and Social Psychology, 104*(4), 716-733.

Lally, P., van Jaarsveld, C. H. M., Potts, H. W. W. and Wardle, J. (2010), How are habits formed: Modelling habit formation in the real world. Eur. J. Soc. Psychol., 40: 998–1009.

Buijze, G. A., Sierevelt, I. N., van der Heijden, B. C. J. M., Dijkgraaf, M. G., & Frings-Dresen, M. H. W. (2016). The Effect of Cold Showering on Health and Work: A Randomized Controlled Trial. *PLoS ONE, 11*(9), e0161749. http://doi.org/10.1371/journal.pone.0161749

Siems, W.G., Brenke R., Sommerburg O., Grune T. (1999). Improved antioxidative protection in winter swimmers. *QJM An International Journal of Medicine.* Apr;92(4):193-8.

Shevchuk N.A. (2008). Adapted cold shower as a potential treatment for depression. *Medical Hypotheses, 70* (5), pp. 995-1001.

Maslow, A. H. (1943). A theory of human motivation. *Psychological Review, 50*(4), 370-396.

Current World Population. (n.d.). Retrieved November 01, 2017, from http://www.worldometers.info/world-population/

Fuller, S. (n.d.). Topic: Health & Fitness Clubs. Retrieved November 02, 2017, from https://www.statista.com/topics/1141/health-and-fitness-clubs/

Sjöström, L., Göran, G., Marcin, K., Alfred, L. (1980). Peripheral insulin in response to the sight and smell of food. *Metabolism-Clinical and Experimental,* Volume 29, Issue 10, 901 – 909.

Tonosaki, K., Hori, Y., Shimzu, Y., Tonosaki, K., (2007). Relationships between insulin release and taste. *Biomedical Research,* Vol. 28, No. 2, 79-83.

Kohlmeier, M. (2015). *Nutrient metabolism: handbook of nutrients.* London: Academic Press.

Reticular Activating System: Definition & Function. (n.d.). Retrieved November 02, 2017, from http://study.com/academy/lesson/reticular-activating-system-definition-function.html

ABOUT THE AUTHOR

Kevin Armentrout is a former United States Marine and a decorated combat veteran. He was awarded the Bronze Star Medal and the Navy and Marine Corps Commendation Medal for heroic actions during combat operations in Al Anbar, Iraq. Kevin has been a leader in the fitness industry as a master trainer and sports nutritionist. He has traveled the world in part to leadership development and been a recurring guest motivational speaker for renowned life and business strategist Tony Robbins. He provides dynamic coaching strategies towards health and fitness to achieve a Relentless State of Mind.

Kevin was born and raised in Lakeland, Florida where he joined the Marine Corps directly after high school in 1998. He served as the commander of a quick reaction force, an assault breacher, and a close quarters battle team leader. After nine years of service, he went on to be a small unit tactics instructor, a foreign weapons expert, and a cultural advisor for military training and operations. Kevin is now a full-time writer, health coach, and public speaker. He lives in Las Vegas with his wife and daughter.

CPSIA information can be obtained
at www.ICGtesting.com
Printed in the USA
BVOW08*0713020318
509339BV00003B/98/P